Family Hiking
in the Smokies

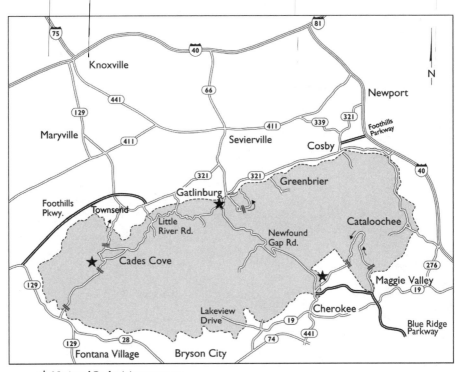

★ National Park visitor centers

Family Hiking in the Smokies

TIME WELL SPENT

HAL HUBBS, CHARLES MAYNARD, AND DAVID MORRIS

Fifth Edition

Knoxville / The University of Tennessee Press

Library of Congress Cataloging-in-Publication Data

Hubbs, Hal.
Family hiking in the Smokies: time well spent / Hal Hubbs, Charles
Maynard, and David Morris. — 5th ed.
p. cm.
Includes index.

ISBN-13: 978-1-62190-578-3 (pbk.)
ISBN-10: 1-62190-578-0 (pbk.)

1. Hiking—Great Smoky Mountains (N.C. and Tenn.)—Guidebooks.
2. Trails—Great Smoky Mountains National Park (N.C. and
   Tenn.)—Guidebooks.
3. Great Smoky Mountains (N.C. and Tenn.)—Guidebooks.
4. Family recreation—Great Smoky Mountains National Park
   (N.C. and Tenn.)—Guidebooks.
I. Hubbs, Hal.
II. Maynard, Charles.
III. Morris, David.
IV. Title.

GV199.42.G73H83 2020
796.52209768'89—dc22
2009020141

John Finley Morris (1983–2011).

As we release this fifth edition of our family hiking guide, it's easy to reflect on the first edition that was originally printed in 1991. That first edition was written out of the desire for a hiking guide of the Smokies that addressed the unique needs of hiking with children of various ages. Over the past thirty years, *Family Hiking in the Smokies* has more than doubled from the original twenty-five hikes to the fifty-two in this current edition. Our children have been the primary motivation and continued inspiration for starting and continuing the production of this guide.

It is with great appreciation and fondest memories that we dedicate this fifth edition to our children: Will Hubbs, Caroline Maynard Lamar, Anna Maynard Lee, Chris Morris, Brian Morris, Ben Morris, and in loving memory of John Morris.

Through all these years and editions, our greatest pleasure has come from hiking with our children into adulthood and watch them "take up the pack" and share hiking adventures with their children. Our hope is that this guide (and future editions) will provide guidance and enjoyment for generations to come!

Contents

Tips for Family Hiking xiii
Great Smoky Mountains National Park xix

BIG CREEK–CATALOOCHEE

1. Midnight Hole and Mouse Creek Falls. 3
2. Mount Sterling 4
3. Little Cataloochee 6
4. Boogerman Loop. 7
5. Woody House. 10
6. Cataloochee Valley Walk 11

COSBY

7. Hen Wallow Falls. 17
8. Mount Cammerer 18
9. Albright Grove 20

GATLINBURG–MOUNT LECONTE

10. Ramsey Cascades 26
11. Porters Creek and Fern Branch Falls 27
12. Gatlinburg Trail 29
13. Sugarlands Valley 30
14. Old Sugarlands 31
15. Cataract Falls. 33
16. Twin Creeks 34
17. Rainbow Falls 35
18. Grotto Falls and Brushy Mountain 36
19. Baskins Creek Falls 38
20. Chimney Tops. 42
21. Alum Cave and Arch Rock to Mount LeConte 44

ELKMONT–METCALF BOTTOMS

22. Laurel Falls–Cove Mountain Fire Tower 50
23. Jakes Creek Falls 52
24. Little River and Cucumber Gap 53
25. Huskey Branch Falls 54
26. Curry Mountain 55
27. Little Greenbrier School and
    Walker Sisters' House 56
28. Upper Meigs Falls 59

NEWFOUND GAP–CLINGMANS DOME

29. Charlies Bunion and the Jumpoff 65
30. Clingmans Dome 68
31. Andrews Bald 69

CADES COVE–TOWNSEND

32. Chestnut Top 73
33. Spruce Flats Falls 73
34. Lynn Camp Prong 76
35. Schoolhouse Gap, Turkeypen Ridge, Finley Cane,
    and Bote Mountain Loop 78
36. John Oliver Place 80
37. Rich Mountain Loop 81
38. Spence Field 82
39. Elijah Oliver Place 84
40. Abrams Falls 85
41. Gregory Bald 87
42. Look Rock Tower 90

CHEROKEE–DEEP CREEK

43. Kephart Prong 94
44. Smokemont Loop 95
45. Oconaluftee Cherokee (Bilingual) 97
46. Flat Creek 98
47. Mingo Falls 99

48. Juney Whank Falls 101

49. Indian Creek Falls. 101

50. Goldmine Loop 103

FONTANA

51. Twentymile Creek Cascade 105

52. Shuckstack Fire Tower 107

Appendix 1. Nature and Historical Trails 109

Appendix 2. Car Travel and Auto Tours 113

Appendix 3. Waterfalls in the Smokies. 117

Appendix 4. Picnicking in the Smokies. 119

Appendix 5. Backpacking with Children 123

Resources 125

Hike Index 129

Mileage Chart 133

Hiking in the mountains is fun but potentially dangerous. Please use every precaution and good sense when visiting the park. Observe all posted warnings and park regulations. The authors and publisher are not responsible for injury, loss, or damage incurred from the use of this guide.

Tips for Family Hiking

The Great Smoky Mountains National Park abounds with opportunities for family recreation. One enjoyable way to experience the park is to walk some of its more than 900 miles of trails. As precious as family leisure time is, it shouldn't be wasted. This book suggests many ways to enjoy the mountains with your family in the limited time you have available.

Family hiking doesn't have to be a frustrating struggle, but it does involve more than just walking a mountain trail. The key to enjoyment is planning ahead.

Most importantly, pick a hike that is suited to your child's abilities. In this book, we've rated hikes according to age ranges. As wonderful as some hikes may be, your preschooler may not be able to make them. The more difficult hikes allow teens to feel a sense of accomplishment. Children who hike a lot may be up to more difficult walks, while an easier hike might be better for kids who have never hiked.

Allow plenty of time. Our time estimates are generous. Most of the enjoyment of a hike should be the actual walk rather than the destination. Your child will remember the experience of being with you longer than the scenery. Relax and walk at your child's pace.

Since children's eyes are closer to the ground, they will see things that you might miss. Be prepared to saunter or you'll seem like a relentless trail boss driving the herd onward. A more relaxed attitude may mean you don't go as far, but the experience with the family is the objective, not the destination.

The old scout motto, "Be Prepared," is a good one for family hiking. Try to think ahead to a child's needs for the entire time on the trail. We always walk with plenty of water and toilet paper (although it seems that if you use less of the former you can use less of the latter). A first aid kit and rain gear are important. Even after starting out on the clearest summer morning, an afternoon thundershower can drench you. It's also nice to have an extra set of clothing in the car.

Wear proper clothing. Remember that mountain temperatures are cooler. The top of the Smokies is in a different climate (closer to that of New England and southern Canada) with weather patterns unlike those of nearby valleys. Keep a jacket in the car in *all* seasons. Allow for wind and rain when choosing what to wear. We often travel with two pairs of shoes and socks, an old pair that can get wet and dirty and a good pair that's left in the car. Always wear athletic shoes or boots, never sandals or flip-flops. Also, loose-fitting play clothes are usually more comfortable for walking. It's difficult to fully enjoy a hike if keeping clothes clean is a priority.

In being prepared, don't overburden yourself. Allow even the youngest to carry some portion of the load. Most children are eager to carry a small pack or fanny pack with part of lunch, the first aid kit, or binoculars. Be prepared, but don't carry the kitchen sink.

Some other things we take are: snacks, small flashlight, magnifying glass, peppermints (or chewing gum), binoculars, flower identification book, water, rain gear, sunscreen, matches, camera/phone (for pictures), and a whistle for each child. Today's mobile phones have great cameras for taking extraordinary photos and videos. However, cellular phones are of little to no use in the park. Cellular service is mostly nonexistent. Do not assume that a cellular phone will be of aid in an emergency. See the list provided below of items we usually take on a hike.

We carry plenty of water because water along the trail is unsafe to drink. Do not drink water from streams or springs. Put an open water bottle filled with water into the freezer the night before a summer hike.

The ice will slowly melt the next day while walking. This will provide cool water along the way. All mountain water must be boiled or chemically treated to be safe. We usually carry water purification tablets for emergencies.

Safety first! A few rules are helpful to keep a hike fun and safe. **Stay on the trail!** This is important for children to understand. It's easy to get lost in a laurel thicket or in dense undergrowth; plus, the forest can be damaged by off-trail walking. Let each child have a whistle to use only in emergencies. (Practice blowing these before you get on the trail.) Tell your children—if you think you are lost, don't wander. Stay still, use the whistle, and listen for searchers.

In case of bathroom emergencies, remember to stay away from water sources. Get off the trail at least 100 feet. Dig a hole six inches deep and cover the hole when finished.

It's fun to hold hands, and essential with younger children, but be mindful of excessive handholding. A child walking with a hand held over the head (even if it is supported) for fifteen or twenty minutes can be most uncomfortable. (Try it yourself.) Some trails allow a family to spread out. **Keep your children in sight** but allow them to go ahead or linger behind.

Pay attention to the signals your child gives you. Stop frequently to rest, play, dawdle, look, and splash. If your child becomes irritable and doesn't want to continue, try distracting him or her with a game. Talk *with* your child, instead of *to* your child. When all else fails, *turn around.* The trick is to anticipate the point of no return before you reach it. (Good luck with that.) Again, pay attention to the signals of your child. It's better to have a pleasant experience on a short walk than a miserable one on a longer trail. You want your child's memory to be of time spent with you in the mountains, rather than time spent being yelled at on the trail.

Use all the senses. Explore smells and textures. While blackberries, blueberries, and other seemingly familiar fruits and fungi might be tempting, it is probably best to avoid tasting anything you encounter on the trail—they may be difficult to clean or may be toxic. Children are apt to learn and remember more through their senses than through the passing on of information. The forest has sounds. Help your children listen quietly for a few minutes every now and then. Sometimes we play listening games. "How many different sounds can you hear?" "How many different birds can you hear?" "How many sounds does a waterfall make?" Try a three- to five-minute silent walk to see what wildlife may be encountered. This can change the routine and may yield some interesting results.

Point out interesting things but be slow to explain. Allow your children to draw their own conclusions. Assist with questions and observations. "What do you think made these rocks smooth?" "How do you think these boulders got here?" "What would it have been like to live in this cabin?" If a child is able, let him or her read brochures and booklets to the whole family. In this way, the child can be the teacher instead of the student.

Creek play is a fun, refreshing way to end a hike. Throwing rocks and sticks into creeks is fun when barefoot and in the water. Be careful of slick rocks and strong current. The water is usually very cold, but children don't seem to mind it as much as adults. Cold water on tired feet feels great. Just remember, turning over rocks disturbs some aquatic inhabitants such as salamanders. Would you want someone to lift the top off your house?

An ice cold drink in a cooler at the car is a wonderful treat! A light snack is also nice to have waiting. These ease the trip back to the motel or home.

The hikes in this book are arranged geographically by area. The mileages are approximations, as are the mileage signs in the park. The Hike Index in the back of the book provides an easy way to identify features of individual hikes. These are our favorites; we hope you enjoy them.

We've included interesting stories, natural features, and points of interest. Our goal is for families to enjoy the Great Smoky Mountains National Park together. The experience of being there with your children can be a most enjoyable one, with patience and a little planning. Truly, Time Well Spent!

SUGGESTED ITEMS FOR SAFE FAMILY HIKING

- Plenty of Water
- Snacks, Chewing Gum, or Hard Candies
- Appropriate Footwear—Such as Athletic Shoes, Boots, Water Shoes — Not Flip-Flops or Slick-Soled Shoes!
- Toilet Paper or Tissues
- Sunscreen
- Small First Aid Kit
- Rain Gear
- Whistle for Each Child
- Flashlight
- Waterproof Matches

- Water-Purification Tablets, Water Filter, or Water Filter Straws
- Extra Clothing
- Extras to Add Interest—Field Guides (Wildflowers, Birds, Plants, etc.), Magnifying Glass, Binoculars, and Camera/ Phone for Pictures
- Garbage Bags—Used for Trash, Waterproof Seat, Rain Gear, or Pack Cover

SMALL FIRST AID KIT

- Adhesive Strip Bandages
- Sterile Gauze Pads
- Adhesive Tape
- Alcohol Pads
- Antiseptic Cream
- Moleskin to prevent blisters
- Children's and Adult Pain Reliever
- Knife with Scissors and Tweezers
- After Bite® for Insect Bites
- "Space" Blanket for Emergency Warmth

SAFETY AND SMOKY MOUNTAIN WEATHER

Before heading out for your adventure, it's a great idea to check a current weather report, as well as informing someone of where you will be. Current weather conditions and forecasts for the Smokies can be obtained at the park visitor centers, or by visiting https://www.nps.gov/grsm/. Mountain weather can vary greatly from surrounding foothills and valleys, especially at higher elevations.

Rainfall. . . . The Smokies usually get about twice the amount of rainfall as surrounding areas, much of which falls in the summer months during thunderstorms. Strong winds, lightning, hail, and heavy rainfall can accompany these storms. Considerable exposure to these elements is possible on many of the trails, particularly in higher elevations. Be ready to take cover in a safe area if you get caught in a sudden storm. Be aware that some trails have steel cables attached to the rock. It is advisable to stay clear of these during thunderstorms as they can increase the chance of lightning strikes. Heavy rain and strong winds can increase

the chance of falling trees. Watch closely for any toppling trees and be prepared to take cover. Landslides are also possible in severe conditions.

Another concern with heavy rainfall is sudden rising water in streams and creeks in the mountains. A footlog (a footbridge made of a single hewn log) can be swept away by this swiftly flowing water. Never attempt to cross a rapidly flowing, swollen stream; it can be extremely dangerous. Consider an alternate route, even if it involves a longer walk.

Snow and Ice. . . . During the winter months, snow and ice are possible even when there is none at lower elevations. Both can be very treacherous while hiking on mountain trails. Snow can melt on warm days, run down trails, and freeze at night, creating dangerous stretches of ice. Attempting to cross these areas of ice without crampons or other proper ice spikes can be extremely dangerous and is not advisable. Information about trail conditions can be obtained at park visitor centers.

Always be aware that extreme changes in weather conditions can occur suddenly. The best preparation is to be well informed. Use common sense and make safe, logical decisions. Changing your destination or delaying your trip can be a very wise choice in certain conditions.

Great Smoky Mountains National Park

Great Smoky Mountains National Park is the most visited national park in the United States, with over 10 million visitors each year. Biodiversity is one of the hallmarks that draws people from all over the world to this mountain sanctuary. Elevations span from 800 feet above sea level to 6,643 feet, creating climate zones in the park that vary from typical local Tennessee weather to conditions similar to southern Canada. More than 700 miles of streams provide habitat for fish, amphibians, insects, and other animals.

The park is a botanical wonder with over 1,600 flowering plant, 50 fern, 100 native tree, and 100 native shrub species. Also at home in the area are 65 mammal, 240 bird, 67 native fish, and over 80 reptile and amphibian species. The Smokies is known as "the Salamander Capital of the World" with over 30 species of the amphibians.

Several species of animals have been reintroduced into the Smokies. The peregrine falcon, otter, brook trout, and elk, which were once natives, are finding a home here again. A small part of the spruce-fir forest endangered by a tiny aphid is being treated to preserve the trees. These efforts are among many that are ongoing in the park. The eastern hemlock, a very common tree in the middle to lower elevations, is under attack from another insect called the hemlock woolly adelgid. Dead hemlock trees are common throughout the park.

The story of the Great Smoky Mountains began about 310–245 million years ago when movements in the earth's crust thrust up rock formed 800–545 million years ago into enormous mountains. Over millions of years, wind and rain wore the mighty mountains down. Too far south for the glacial forces of the ice age, the Smokies became a haven for northern flora and fauna such as spruce-fir trees.

Indigenous people arrived in the area only about 9,000–12,000 years ago. The Cherokee were the last American Indians to live and hunt in the Smokies. European settlers immigrated to the area in the late 1700s and early 1800s, pressuring the Cherokee out. The forcible removal of the Cherokee became known as the Trail of Tears. One in four Cherokee died on the trail to the Indian Territory (Oklahoma) during this dark time in the history of the region. To avoid removal, some Cherokee found refuge in the Smokies where their descendants remain to this day.

Settlers of European descent moved into the valleys and coves to farm and herd. In the late 1800s and early 1900s, logging and mining came to the Great Smokies. Many worked as loggers, miners, railroaders, and suppliers. In the 1920s, concern for preserving the area arose. The National Park Service was started in 1916, and the Appalachian Trail (over 2,100 miles from Georgia to Maine) was constructed in the 1920s and 1930s. Although many people worked tirelessly to establish a national park in the Smokies, many families' homes were sacrificed for the park to come into being.

The Great Smoky Mountains National Park is an international biosphere reserve that attempts to preserve geological, biological, and botanical diversity as well as human history. Many people never get out of the car as they visit the park. However, the Park Service provides excellent opportunities to experience the Great Smoky Mountains in a more complete way.

The three visitor centers are great places to start your experience. Each offers a theme highlighting a different aspect of the Smokies. At Sugarlands, near Gatlinburg, a museum and movie introduce visitors to the diversity of plant and animal life. The life of the early settlers can be better understood with a visit to Oconaluftee, near Cherokee. The Cades Cove Visitor Center offers a close look at a mill and life on a mountain cove farm, with many interpretive programs.

At each of the visitor centers is a resource center operated by the Great Smoky Mountains Association. Most of the books on the resource list in the back of this book can be purchased there, along with other materials such as DVDs, posters, maps, CDs, and gifts. All purchases benefit the park. A valuable resource at the visitor centers is the park newspaper, *Smokies Guide*. It lists the many programs in the park, including ranger-led activities, which are free of charge. Brochures and booklets about various aspects of the park are also available for a small charge.

Ten campgrounds provide beautiful settings for overnight stays within the park. Visitors pay a nominal fee at the entrance to the campground before setting up camp. Some campgrounds are closed in the winter. Popular sites can be difficult to get into in the summer. Cades Cove, Smokemont, and Elkmont require reservations in the summer months. Others are filled on a first-come, first-served basis. Also, horseback riding is available in the park through authorized concessions.

Check at a visitor center for more information or online at https://www
.nps.gov/grsm/.

The picnic areas in the park provide clean restrooms, picnic tables,
and fire grates at scenic spots. Most are closed in the winter but are wonderful places to enjoy a meal in the other seasons.

Ask a ranger for a Junior Ranger booklet. The Junior Ranger program is open to children ages 8–12. Children who complete the activities
in the booklet and meet the necessary requirements will earn a Junior
Ranger badge or pin.

The self-guided nature and auto trails are other ways to get a closer
look at the wonders of the Smokies. Try one of the Quiet Walkways that
are located throughout the park and are less than a half mile long. You'll
see and enjoy more when you drive slowly and get out of the car often.

The Spring Wildflower Pilgrimage is held every year for a week near
the end of April. Hikes, programs, motorcades, and children's activities
are offered each spring. Write or ask at a park visitor center for more
information (www.wildflowerpilgrimage.org). The city of Pigeon Forge
hosts Wilderness Wildlife Week each year. Talks, programs, and hikes for
all ages are offered free of charge. Check with the city of Pigeon Forge for
more information. Several other special events are held at Oconaluftee,
Cades Cove, and Sugarlands. Information is available in the park's newspaper, *Smokies Guide*, online at https://www.smokiesinformation.org
/official-park-newspaper, or at the visitor centers.

It can be difficult to have time for a vacation or a day off. When that
time does become available, it's best to spend it wisely. We hope that
families will have a good experience in the Great Smoky Mountains National Park—and enjoy Time Well Spent.

A WORD ABOUT WILDLIFE AND PLANTS

Aside from the beautiful vistas, the wildlife and plants found in the Great
Smoky Mountains National Park make it unique. In fact, many people
visit only to catch a glimpse of a bear or an elk, or to see wildflowers in
bloom. Animals and plants in any ecosystem are in a delicate balance;
with millions visiting the Smokies each year, a disregard for this fact
could spell disaster.

The following are some tips to ensure the beauty of the Smoky Mountains (whatever you perceive it to be) will be around for our children and
grandchildren to enjoy.

- Always stay on maintained trails; leaving the trail may damage young plants or disrupt nesting animals.

- Never approach wildlife, not even deer or chipmunks.

- Never entice animals with food; this can cause immediate danger to you and long-term danger to the animals. (Hence the slogan—A Fed Bear is a Dead Bear!)

- If you are fortunate enough to see a bear or an elk, enjoy it from a distance; if you meet one on a trail, give it plenty of room.

- Never leave food or packs unattended. If a bear approaches during a picnic, quickly gather everything and move away.

- Only two species of poisonous snakes are found in the Great Smoky Mountains National Park, the Timber Rattlesnake and the Northern Copperhead. Although snake encounters are rare, use caution. Stay on the trail and keep a watchful eye when crossing logs or brush.

- Never attempt to cross a stream in high water. An afternoon thunderstorm can cause a creek to temporarily overrun banks that contained it earlier in the day.

- Enjoy the beauty of wildflowers by lingering or taking pictures, but never pick or damage plants in any way; this is a federal offense.

- Report any aggressive animals or dangerous situations at the nearest ranger station or visitor center.

Enjoy hiking, but as always, use common sense.

Family Hiking
in the Smokies

Big Creek–Cataloochee

The Big Creek–Cataloochee areas are some of the most scenic in the entire park. Big Creek is popular due to its proximity to Interstate 40, while Cataloochee is an undiscovered treasure found by few. Both can be seen in a day trip or enjoyed for longer periods by staying at a campground in either area.

From the Walnut Bottom area to its junction with the Pigeon River, Big Creek drops 1,200 feet (120 stories), or an average of 200 feet per mile. The change in elevation produces many beautiful cascades and small falls on this large creek.

The Big Creek Basin was logged by the Crestmont Lumber Company in the early 1900s. Many of the trails follow old logging railroad beds. Evidence of the logging days can be found—steel cables, rails, spikes, and old roadbeds. The forest, mostly hardwoods and spruce-fir, has recovered well from the extensive logging.

To reach Big Creek, take the Waterville Exit 451 on I-40, about 65 miles east of Knoxville or 50 miles west of Asheville. Cross the Pigeon River and turn left at the end of the bridge (the Appalachian Trail passes over this bridge). Follow the road past the Walters Power Plant, where river adventure companies have a raft launch on the Pigeon River. Continue past the power plant to an intersection 2 miles from the interstate. Continue straight at the four-way stop up a narrow road to the ranger station. The picnic area and campground, which are closed in the winter, are about 0.6 miles beyond the ranger station.

At the eastern end of the Great Smoky Mountains National Park, a remote valley offers tales of the past and hope for the future. As the 1900s began, Cataloochee was the largest community in the Smokies with some 200 buildings. The valley was once owned by Colonel Robert Love, a land speculator. As the area around Cataloochee grew, Colonel Love granted homesteads to those who agreed to settle and improve the land. Some of the early families were Caldwell, Hannah, Bennett, Noland, Palmer, Franklin, Woody, and Barnes. Descendants of these families lived in the area as late as the 1960s. The name Cataloochee comes from the Cherokee *Gadalutsi* meaning "fringe standing erect." This was probably a reference to the trees growing along the side of the mountains and atop the narrow, steep ridges. Numerous opportunities for hiking, picnicking, and sightseeing are available in Cataloochee.

Elk were reintroduced to the park in Cataloochee Valley in 2001 and 2002. Since that time the elk herd in the experimental release has increased. Elk once lived in the mountains, but by the late 1700s, they had been crowded out due to hunting and loss of habitat. The best time to see these large, majestic creatures is in the early morning or early evening. Sometimes on cloudy, rainy days they graze in the large open pastures of the Cataloochee Valley.

Two routes access Cataloochee. Exit I-40 at US 276 (Exit 20; Maggie Valley). Turn right on Cove Creek Road after the interstate exit. The paved road becomes a gravel road after about 4 miles, but pavement resumes after 7.5 miles from the interstate, or 2 miles beyond the park boundary. The 11 miles from the interstate to Cataloochee is a scenic drive.

The other route begins at Big Creek. Take I-40 to Exit 451 (Waterville). Follow the directions given above toward the Big Creek Ranger

Station. At the intersection, 2 miles from the interstate, turn left onto NC 284. This well-maintained gravel road leads 16 miles to Cataloochee. Do not expect to go faster than 20 mph on this road. It takes roughly an hour to cover the 16 miles. Sometimes we use one route going in and another coming out. Either way, Cataloochee is a wonderful treat that shouldn't be missed. The campground is closed in winter, but the restrooms there are available year-round.

The cardinal or redbird was called "Daughter of the Sun" by the Cherokee.

1. MIDNIGHT HOLE AND MOUSE CREEK FALLS

4 miles roundtrip

Allow 4 to 5 hours

Elementary schoolers can hike this moderate walk along a beautiful creek to two waterfalls.

How to Get There: Take Exit 451 (the Waterville Exit) on I-40 about 65 miles east of Knoxville and 50 miles west of Asheville. Cross the Pigeon River and turn left at the end of the bridge, over which the Appalachian Trail passes. Follow the road past the Walters Power Plant and go straight at the intersection up the narrow road to the ranger station. The picnic area and campground are about 0.6 miles beyond the ranger station. These are closed in the winter. Pit toilets are available at the parking area near the ranger station, at the picnic area, and at the campground.

Description of the Hike: The walk is on the Big Creek Trail, which begins near the Big Creek Picnic Area. The trail is a wide roadbed making it easy to walk side by side. The gain in elevation is slight, so the walk is not strenuous. The trail is open to hikers and horses and is popular, especially with fishermen.

Initially the campground can be seen far below on the left. At about 0.2 miles, a steep side trail comes up from the campground. Shortly after the side trail, Big Creek can be seen below. Notice the change in rocks along the trail as you pass over the Greenbrier Fault. The stratified Rich

Butt stone gives way to the more solid and fine-grained Thunderhead Sandstone. By the time you reach the creek, all the rock is Thunderhead Sandstone.

At 1.4 miles from the campground, is Midnight Hole, a large pool filled with the clear water of Big Creek. Appropriately named, Midnight Hole pool is dark green in the winter and dark as midnight in the summer. Enormous boulders squeeze Big Creek into a small opening through which two 8-foot waterfalls pour. In wet weather, water spills over the rock that divides the two falls to form a single waterfall. At Midnight Hole are remnants of the logging industry that worked this area in the past. Steel cable and rails can be seen in the woods and among the rocks. This is a wonderful place for a picnic, a nice rest, or a pretty photo.

Continue up the trail 0.6 miles beside the roaring Big Creek to Mouse Creek Falls. A hitching rail on the left marks the place to walk over to view the falls. Boulders provide a pleasant place to observe the beautiful 50-foot hourglass cascade at the mouth of Mouse Creek. Several streams intertwine to form a wide base of falling water. A small pool at the base slows the water as it crosses an old logging railroad bed before reaching Big Creek.

The return to your car is easy and allows for another opportunity to look at Midnight Hole. This walk is fine in any season. Just remember that in winter the gate may be closed on the road to the picnic area and campground; thus, 1.2 miles will be added to the roundtrip mileage.

2. MOUNT STERLING

5.4 miles roundtrip

Allow 5 to 6 hours

Older elementary schoolers and **teens** will be challenged by this difficult walk up through the spruce-fir forest to a fire tower.

How to Get There: The trailhead is about 9 miles from Exit 451 (Waterville) on I-40. At Exit 451, cross the Pigeon River and turn left at the end of the bridge. Drive 2 miles to the intersection with NC 284 and turn left. Drive 6.7 miles to Mt. Sterling Gap. The trail is on the right side of the road.

Description of the Hike: Begin at the trailhead at Mt. Sterling Gap on NC 284. The trail starts on an old roadbed that once supplied the fire tower with provisions. Mt. Sterling Gap was an important pass for thousands of years. Buffalo, elk, and deer used the pass even before humans walked through the mountains on the trail. American Indians also used this trail for thousands of years. Bishop Francis Asbury, a Methodist circuit rider, passed through the gap in 1810 on his way from Tennessee into North Carolina.

The entire hike to the tower is uphill, gaining about 2,000 feet in 2.7 miles. At 0.5 miles, the trail meets the Long Bunk Trail, which goes left to Little Cataloochee. The trail passes through a northern hardwood forest with some large oaks. On the ascent are a few good views of Cataloochee Valley and of Mt. Sterling.

The trail reaches the crest of Mt. Sterling at 2.3 miles. Turn right onto the Mt. Sterling Ridge Trail and continue for 0.4 miles to the Mt. Sterling Fire Tower and Campsite #38. The sixty-foot tower, which stands at 5,820 feet above sea level, was built in 1934. Fire towers are no longer used to watch for forest fires, but this tower is used as a radio repeater in the Park Service's park-wide radio system.

The start of a family hike to Mt. Sterling and one of the last towers in the park.

The views from the tower are amazing. To the north is Mt. Cammerer and Mt. Guyot with Little Cataloochee and Cataloochee Valley to the south. Few traces of human habitation can be seen from this remote spot. Although the tower is difficult to get to, it is a wonderful experience of wilderness.

We recommend returning by the same route you came, for a round-trip of 5.4 miles. However, an alternative downward route is possible by way of the Baxter Creek Trail, which descends 6.1 miles from the fire tower to Big Creek Campground. The Baxter Creek Trail is a steep, long trail for the very adventurous. This trip would require a second car.

3. LITTLE CATALOOCHEE

5.4 miles roundtrip

Allow 4 hours

Older elementary schoolers and **teens** will like this trail that traverses back in time to historic buildings and ruins. It also offers wildflowers, creeks, and fall colors.

How to Get There: There are two ways to reach this trailhead. **Route One**—After leaving I-40 at Exit 20, turn onto Cove Creek Road and drive about 6 miles to the park boundary. Drive down the gravel road about 2 miles to the Cataloochee Road. Cross the paved road and continue on the gravel road for about 2 miles; then turn to the right. At about 3.5 miles from the intersection, the trailhead is on the left (5.7 miles from the paved road or 13.3 miles from the interstate).

Route Two—The trailhead is about 11.5 miles from Exit 451 (Waterville) on I-40. At Exit 451, cross the Pigeon River and turn left at the end of the bridge. In 2 miles, turn left onto NC 284 and drive 6.7 miles to Mt. Sterling Gap. The trail is on the right side of the road about 2.5 miles past Mt. Sterling Gap.

Description of the Hike: The trail begins on NC 284. Head downhill on an old roadbed to a bridge crossing Correll Branch. As the trail climbs along the side of a ridge, the sound of Little Cataloochee Creek can be heard far below. At 1.1 miles, the trail intersects with Long Bunk Trail, which goes to the right. The Hannah Cemetery is 0.2 miles up the Long Bunk Trail. Continue on the Little Cataloochee Trail to the Hannah

Cabin, which is off to the right at 1.2 miles (only 0.1 miles from the junction with Long Bunk Trail).

The Hannah Cabin was built by John Jackson Hannah in 1864. Notice the puncheon floor with some puncheons being nearly 30 inches wide. A puncheon is a log flattened on one side by an adze, while the bottom is still rounded. The Hannah Cabin has a chimney built with handmade brick from local clay. The National Park Service restored this cabin in 1976.

The trail continues across Little Cataloochee Creek to the old community of Ola. Will Messer had an eleven-room house in Ola, and the community was named for his daughter, Viola. A post office and store served the Little Cataloochee area. Evidence of the settlement is all about—clearings, a spring, apple trees, and fence posts.

Move up hill to the Little Cataloochee Baptist Church, 2 miles from the trailhead. This structure was built in 1889 by the local people, including Will Messer. Go inside the church, and wander through the cemetery just below the church. Make a rubbing with charcoal and paper of some of the tombstones. The Woodys, Hannahs, Messers, and Cooks are among the families that once inhabited the valley.

About 0.7 miles beyond the church, is the Dan Cook Cabin, built by Dan Cook in the late 1850s. The cabin was reconstructed in 1999 through a grant to the Friends of the Smokies and the National Park Foundation from the makers of Log Cabin Syrup. Across from the cabin are the ruins of an apple barn used by Will Messer, who married Dan Cook's daughter, Rachel. Rest at the cabin before returning along the same route to your car. This is a wonderful hike to get a sense of those who once lived here and farmed in the area.

4. BOOGERMAN LOOP

7.7 miles or 9.8 miles roundtrip

Allow 5 to 7 hours

Teens will find this hike through old-growth forest and old house sites a challenge. The trail climbs about 1,000 feet in 2.7 miles, steeply at times.

How to Get There: The trailhead (Caldwell Fork Trail) is on the Cataloochee Road about 300 yards past the campground. Limited parking is available at the trailhead. Restrooms are in the campground.

Elk

Elk, the largest of the deer family, once grazed throughout the Smokies. By the late 1700s, settlers had hunted and virtually removed elk from their natural habitat. Since the National Park Service's mission is to preserve native plants and animals, they decided to reintroduce elk into the Smokies. Since 2001 the National Park Service has released over fifty elk in Cataloochee Valley.

As with any wildlife reintroduction, time is critical for adaptation to a new environment. After a slow start, the elk population has steadily increased over the past few years, with some moving into the Oconaluftee area. Now elk can be seen not only in Cataloochee Valley, but in the fields near Oconaluftee Visitor Center, as well as along Balsam Mountain Road off the Blue Ridge Parkway. The best times to view elk are early morning and late evening just before dark.

* **Caution** when viewing elk (and all wildlife) cannot be over emphasized here! *Never* approach elk! *Observe* all warnings. Fields will be closed when elk are present. Remember, many rewarding experiences can be enjoyed from the safety of your vehicle. Be considerate of others and use designated pull-offs for viewing. Binoculars and spotting scopes will enhance your viewing experience.

Elk.

Description of the Hike: Begin the walk on the Caldwell Fork Trail by crossing Palmer Creek on a long footlog. Caldwell Fork empties into Palmer Creek to the left of the trailhead to form Cataloochee Creek. Initially the trail follows Caldwell Fork through a flat area of large pine trees with rhododendron growing along the creek. Enjoy the soft path paved with pine needles underfoot.

Caldwell Fork was named for one of the families that lived along this beautiful creek. After 0.5 miles, the pine forest gives way to old-growth hemlock, which are currently under attack by the hemlock woolly adelgid. Many of these large trees are dead or dying. At 0.8 miles, after the trail crosses Caldwell Fork on a footlog, turn left onto the Boogerman Trail.

The Boogerman Trail gets its name from Robert Palmer. It is said that Palmer was a very shy child who, when asked his name in school, hid his face and replied, "I'm the Boogerman"—thus the nickname. When the valley became too crowded for him, Palmer used hand tools to build a road to this remote area. He never allowed timber to be cut on his land.

The next 2.7 miles of the Boogerman Trail are uphill through the area that Palmer farmed. The first 2-mile stretch follows Palmer's old hand-cut roadbed and then the trail narrows. Notice the large trees that still stand on Palmer's old place. These trees remain because Palmer's land was spared from logging. The trail climbs Den Ridge and crosses Palmer Branch to an area of second-growth trees. This was Palmer's home place, which consisted of two cabins, barns, and other outbuildings.

After Palmer's homestead, the trail descends slightly and then resumes climbing. Near the top of the climb, the trail crosses over Sag Branch. After reaching the highest point, the trail then descends toward Caldwell Fork. On the way down, the Boogerman Trail crosses Snake Branch a few times. You will pass through a farmstead with remnants of fence posts and old stone walls. At 3.8 miles from the trailhead, a side trail passes through a house site to the Messer Cemetery, which is surrounded by a barbed wire fence. After 4.1 miles, the Boogerman Trail eventually loops back to reconnect with the Caldwell Fork Trail.

At this point, you have three options to complete the hike. One option is to turn right and go down the Caldwell Fork Trail. On the map this is the shortest and most obvious way back to your car. It is only 2 miles from where you left the Caldwell Fork Trail to walk on the Boogerman Trail. However, there are numerous *wet* crossings of Caldwell Fork with no footlogs. In high water, these crossings are dangerous and should *not* be attempted. In the heat of summer, these crossings can be refreshing, but you must pay attention to the water level. Although this is the shortest return to your car, it is not the easiest or safest. We recommend either of the two options below.

A second option is to turn left onto Caldwell Fork Trail and walk 0.5 miles to the Big Fork Ridge Trail. Turn right and walk 3.2 miles over Big Fork Ridge to the Cataloochee Road. Turn right on Cataloochee Road and walk 2.3 miles back to your car. This route makes a 7.7-mile loop. This is a great hike. You will pass where the elk were reintroduced to Cataloochee Valley in 2001. Plus, you will see some of the historic buildings of the valley.

A third option is simply to turn around and return the way you came. This route makes the hike 9.8 miles and requires climbing back up over the ridge. This makes for a long day and plenty of climbing.

As difficult as Boogerman Trail is, it is an amazing place with old house sites, stone walls, cemeteries, and old-growth, giant trees. We think it is well worth the effort, but not for the faint of heart. Even teens with experience will find this amazing trail a challenge.

5. WOODY HOUSE

2 miles roundtrip

Allow 1.5 to 2 hours

Elementary schoolers will enjoy this walk to an old house and springhouse along Rough Fork. See spring wildflowers and possibly deer and elk on this wonderful walk on an old roadbed.

How to Get There: Begin this walk at the upper end of the Cataloochee Valley, which is 12 miles from Exit 20 on I-40 in North Carolina. After leaving I-40 at Exit 20, turn onto Cove Creek Road and drive about 6 miles to the park boundary. Drive about 2 miles more down the gravel road and turn left onto the paved Cataloochee Road. Drive down into Cataloochee Valley. At the end of the paved road, continue past Palmer Chapel. Turn left, go over the bridge, and drive to the end of the road. You will pass the Caldwell House and Barn. The trailhead is beyond the gate at the end of the road. The parking area is on the right. The nearest restrooms are the restrooms near the church or the restrooms at the Cataloochee Campground.

Description of the Hike: The trail follows an old roadbed along Rough Fork to the Woody House. The trail crosses the stream three times on footlogs. The original house was a log building constructed in the late 1800s, but as the Woody family grew, the house was enlarged. The original log structure is underneath the siding on the right side of the house. Notice the thickness of the window frames in that part of the house compared to the other window frames. The front window was once the front door to the cabin.

Today the house and springhouse are all that is left of the once large farm that sprawled along the creek and over the ridges. Keep your eyes open for the elk that share this beautiful valley with deer and bear. Visit Palmer Chapel, Oak Grove School House, and Caldwell House while seeing Cataloochee Valley.

6. CATALOOCHEE VALLEY WALK

8.4 miles roundtrip or any distance you choose

Allow 4 to 5 hours

Children of all ages can do pieces of this walk. Several herds of elk can often be seen in the open fields. The best chance of seeing elk is early in the morning or just before sunset. They will often be out on cool, rainy days. In the winter when the leaves are off the trees, the elk are usually present for much of the day. An old house, church, school, and barns remain from the thriving Cataloochee community before the national park was created in the early 1930s.

How to Get There: Take the Cataloochee Road down into the valley. After the bridge over Cataloochee Creek, turn right onto a dirt/gravel road. Drive 0.5 miles to the Palmer Place. Or to access other parts of the valley, simply drive straight after crossing the bridge. Restrooms are in the campground, at Palmer Place, and just beyond Palmer Chapel.

Description of the Hike: This walk can begin anywhere in Cataloochee Valley. One way we enjoy the valley is to drive from one end to the other before starting the walk. Depending upon the weather, where the elk are, how the family has done with the drive into the valley, we then decide how much to walk. The following description begins at the lower end and works toward the upper end. However, begin and end at any point

How Deer Got Antlers
A Cherokee Legend

Long ago, deer had no antlers. The buck had a smooth head like the doe. Deer was a swift runner and Rabbit was a great jumper. Many of the animals wanted to know which of the two could go farthest at the same time. The animals decided to have a contest, and a fine set of antlers was fashioned and offered as the prize. On the appointed day, all the animals gathered at the edge of a large thicket.

The race was to go through the thicket to the forest on the other side and then back through the thicket. Before the race began, Rabbit asked if he could go through the thicket to find his way, saying he wasn't familiar with the area. Deer and the other animals agreed that this was fair.

However, Rabbit was gone such a long time that he was suspected of deceit. He was known for his trickery. After a little longer, when he still wasn't back, a messenger was sent to find him. The messenger spied Rabbit in the middle of the thicket, clearing a path. The messenger quietly left and told the other animals. When Rabbit returned, the animals accused him of cheating, which he denied. All the animals went into the thicket where they found the cleared road. It was agreed that no trickster deserved the antler prize, and so it was awarded to Deer. To this day, all bucks wear antlers and rabbits gnaw on brush.

you like. Cataloochee is simply a delight in any form or fashion. There are booklets describing the buildings of Cataloochee Valley available at the pull-off near the bridge at Cataloochee Creek as you enter the valley.

Begin at the Palmer House, which contains a small display of the valley's history. Construction of this dogtrot house (two houses under one roof with an open breezeway between them) by Fate Palmer first began in the 1860s. Most likely the house started as a log structure on one side, and then the second side was added as the family grew. Around 1901–1905, the Palmers sided the house with sawed lumber. There is a barn, a springhouse, and a smokehouse at this site. The small bunkhouse

White-tail deer.

across the road was built by the Palmers to house fishermen and tourists in the 1920s. A post office (one of three in the neighborhood) was in the Palmer home.

As you walk up the road, a path leads to the Palmer Cemetery just beyond the barn. Continue up the dirt road to the main paved road. Head to the right and walk past the campground. The Caldwell Fork Trailhead is on the left. A small path follows the left side of the road. The Cataloochee Horse Trail leads off to the left, 1 mile from the Palmer House. The horse trail follows the route of the original road through the valley. It is rough and rocky. It is easier to walk along the paved road. However, if you walk on the horse trail, notice the fence posts are signs of farming from an earlier era.

If you stay on the main road, you will pass the Messer Barn, which was moved from Little Cataloochee by the Park Service in 1977. Will Messer built the barn in the early 1900s. Continue past the ranger station, and you will reach the edge of a large grassy field where elk often graze. On the upper end of the fields, Palmer Chapel Methodist Church is on the left. The congregation dates to the mid-1800s, but the building was constructed in the early 1900s. The one-room church faces the old road and Palmer Creek. Across the road from the church is a steep path to a large cemetery on the ridge.

Just beyond the church is a restroom on the right. Follow the road past the restroom. Go left over the creek. Beech Grove Schoolhouse is 150 yards to the right. In 1901 this building replaced an earlier log structure that had served as the community school. Notice the construction that allowed for the two rooms to become one large room for special occasions, like a spelling bee or school program.

On up the valley, notice two side trails to the Dock Caldwell and Hiram Caldwell Cemeteries. These two family plots hold many of the original families that settled and farmed the valley. The Hiram Caldwell House is on the left with the barn on the right. The house was finished in 1906 and stood as the center of the Caldwell farm. Imagine all the surrounding ridges as pasture or farmland with few to no trees. Sometimes the elk are in the fields on the right. Follow the creek and the road to the gate. The Big Fork Trailhead is to the left just before the end of the road.

To extend the walk through Cataloochee Valley, continue on the old roadbed beyond the gate. The Woody House is 1.1 miles beyond the gate. The trail crosses the creek three times on footlogs. See Hike #5 on page 10 for more information on this hike.

You can return by the same route or take any combination of routes to reach your car. The distances from the Palmer House to various landmarks are listed below. Cataloochee Valley is a favorite place that is not heavily traveled; but do pay attention to road traffic.

Distance in Miles to Landmarks along the Cataloochee Valley Walk

Palmer Place/Restrooms	0.0
Palmer Cemetery	0.1
Cataloochee Road (Main Road)	0.5
Campground/Restrooms	0.7
Caldwell Fork Trailhead	0.8

Horse Trail	1.0
Ranger Station/Messer Barn	1.2
Horse Trail	1.4
Edge of Field (Where Elk Sometimes Graze)	1.6
Palmer Chapel	2.2
Restroom	2.3
Bridge/Beech Grove School	2.4
Dock Caldwell Cemetery Trail	2.5
Hiram Caldwell Cemetery Trail	2.6
Caldwell Place–House/Barn	2.8
Big Fork Trailhead	3.1
Gate at End of Road	3.2
Woody Place	4.3

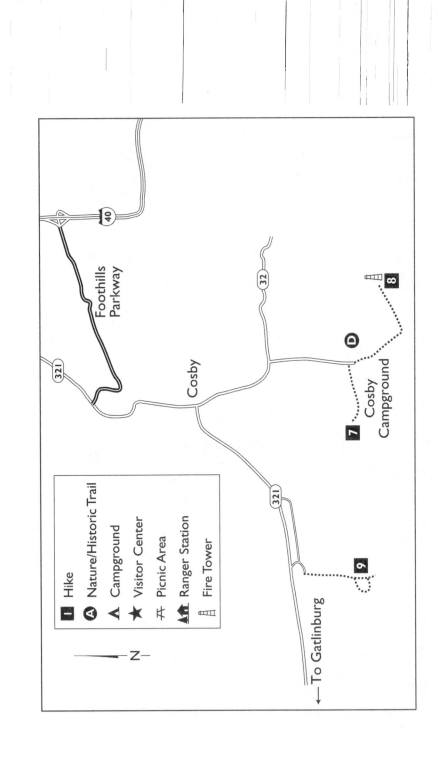

Cosby

The Cosby area is easily accessible. From Gatlinburg, it is 19 miles east on US 321. From I-40, it is 8 miles west on the Foothills Parkway to US 321. From US 321, take TN 32 and drive 1.5 miles to the Cosby park entrance. After turning off TN 32, it is 2 more miles to the Cosby Campground and Picnic Area. Restrooms are available year-round in the picnic area. This campground, although near the interstate (about 11.5 miles), is rarely full. Cosby is a favorite for those who simply want to be away for a weekend.

7. HEN WALLOW FALLS

4.3 miles roundtrip

Allow 2 to 3 hours

Elementary schoolers will enjoy this moderate hike that rises about 700 feet in 2.1 miles. This hike offers a creek, waterfall, and colorful fall leaves.

How to Get There: Hen Wallow Falls is reached via the Gabes Mountain Trail. The trailhead is across the road just below the Cosby Campground and Picnic Area.

Description of the Hike: The first part of the hike is on a slightly rocky roadbed that goes 0.3 miles until a feeder trail from the Cosby Campground enters from the left. Stay to the right and cross Rock Creek on a footlog. The next 0.5-mile stretch winds through a hardwood forest that gives way to rhododendron. A log bench provides an opportunity to rest or play.

At 1.1 miles, a stone footbridge crosses Crying Creek, so named because a man mistakenly shot his brother while the two were on a bear hunt. After 30 yards, continue on the Gabes Mountain Trail to the left. This stretch is a typical mountain trail with loose rocks and plenty of exposed roots; so watch your toes and pick up your feet! A footlog crosses the next creek, and the trail goes to the right. (The trail appears to continue uphill here at the end of the footlog, but it actually goes to the right.) As you pass through Toms Gap, a grave marker for Sally Sutton, a child, is just off the trail to the right. The trail meanders through old home sites around the northeastern slopes of Gabes Mountain before coming to the side trail to Hen Wallow Falls.

The 800-foot side trail descends to the base of the 95-foot-high falls. This part can be tricky for smaller children; so hold onto hands tightly. *Observe the warning signs! Do not climb on the rocks!!* The view to the north (away from the falls) is of Round and Green Mountains. Cosby can be seen in the distance. This is a very enjoyable hike any time of the year. It is cool in the summer and colorful in the fall. Once on a visit here in September, we saw salamanders all over the rocks beside the falls. Follow the same route back to the campground. This trail is a nice complement to the Cosby Nature Trail, which begins at the amphitheater.

8. MOUNT CAMMERER

11 miles roundtrip

Allow 6 to 7 hours

Teens will find this strenuous hike to a mountain peak very challenging. In less than 5 miles, 2,575 feet in altitude is gained. This hike offers fine views, spring flowers, colorful fall leaves, and a fire lookout tower.

How to Get There: This hike starts on the Low Gap Trail, which begins above the group campsites in the Cosby Campground. Park in the lot provided for hikers below the amphitheater.

Description of the Hike: Walk on the paved road past the amphitheater and through the group campground to a graveled pathway. The trail sign points to the Low Gap and Lower Mt. Cammerer Trails. Do not take the Lower Mt. Cammerer Trail for this hike. It is a much longer walk to the fire tower. Continue on the gravel jeep road past the campground water tower. Opposite the water tower, in the woods, are some old stone walls from houses that were part of a settlement. The jeep road ends at the footlog over Cosby Creek. Before the creek crossing, more stone walls are visible.

At the Mt. Cammerer fire tower, one of only five remaining in the park.

The trail gradually ascends through rhododendron as it follows Cosby Creek. The creek is inviting on hot summer days but is calming in any season. Two switchbacks move the trail away from the creek through a boulder field. A small branch flows through a drain tile under the trail. A rhododendron thicket signals a steeper climb to Low Gap.

Look for quartz among the rocks of the trail. Patches of mountain laurel, galax, and ferns dot the higher elevations. Carefully cross the small branch and rest by its waters, because the next part is the steepest yet as the trail climbs to Low Gap through hardwoods. At Low Gap the trail meets the Appalachian Trail (A.T.). Before turning northeast (left) along the A.T., enjoy a respite at the gap. There are oak, silver bell, and sweet birch trees. Sweet birch has black bark with long, pale horizontal lenticels on young trunks and sooty black pates on old trees. When the bark of the twigs is peeled off, it tastes and smells of wintergreen. Mountain people used sweet birch twigs as toothbrushes.

Continue on the A.T. to the northeast going through mountain laurel, rhododendron, and galax. A beech and yellow birch grove is along the way. Yellow birch was used by the settler to make clothespins, toothpicks, and light furniture. The last mile on the A.T. is on a ridgetop through rhododendron. The trail comes to a junction by a stand of yellow birch; the A.T. goes to the right while the Mt. Cammerer Trail goes to the left.

Walk the next 0.6 miles on a ridgeback through spruce, fir, rhododendron, mountain laurel, and galax. Before the top, the trail descends to a small gap with a hitching rail. Climb through the rhododendron to the bare, quartz-streaked metasandstone rocks of the peak. The octagonal fire lookout tower was constructed in the late 1930s of stone and wood. Though no longer in use, it is one of five fire towers remaining in the park.

The fire lookout tower was restored in 1995 by the National Park Service through the efforts of Friends of the Smokies. The wooden catwalk, windows, and roof were replaced. Visitors can go inside the tower and see into the park and far beyond it.

The 5,025-foot Mt. Cammerer is named for Arno B. Cammerer, director of the National Park Service at the creation of the Great Smoky Mountains National Park. Before the peak was named for this Nebraskan, it was called White Rocks by Tennesseans and Sharp Top by North Carolinians.

By whatever name, this peak offers one of the most outstanding views of the Smokies. A 360-degree horizon allows views of Mt. Sterling, Mt. Guyot, Old Black, Cosby, Newport, and even the distant Cumberlands on a clear day. One rainy day, we struggled to the top to be rewarded with clear blue skies above and a sea of white clouds below. Other times the valley can have a nice clear day, while the top is shrouded with fog. In any weather, Mt. Cammerer is a rewarding experience year-round. Climbing it and the return takes a full day, so get an early start. The effort is certainly worth it.

9. ALBRIGHT GROVE

6.8 miles roundtrip

Allow 4 to 5 hours

Elementary schoolers can walk this moderate hike that gains 1,300 feet in 3 miles and offers old-growth forest, a log cabin, a creek, and spring wildflowers.

How to Get There: The trailhead is off US 321 between Gatlinburg and Cosby. Turn east at traffic light #3 in Gatlinburg onto US 321. Go 15.8

miles (3.6 miles west of Cosby) to Baxter Road. Follow this road until it
ends at Laurel Springs Road. Turn right and follow the gravel road 100
yards. The Maddron Bald Trail begins at a gated roadbed on the left.
When parking, do not block the entrance to the trail. The nearest public
restrooms are at the Cosby Campground 5 miles away.

Description of the Hike: The first 2.3 miles of the Maddron Bald Trail
is an easy walk on a jeep road, which is also used for horses. The initial
0.7-mile climb goes through poplar and hardwood with a rhododendron
understory. The old Willis Baxter cabin, built around 1889, stands 0.7
miles from the gate. The cabin is said to have been built from the wood
of one chestnut tree. The small cabin was home for an entire family until
a larger house was built a short distance away.

From the cabin the climb is a little steeper. At 1.2 miles, the trail intersects the Gabes Mountain and Old Settlers Trails. To the left, it is

Stands of virgin tim-
ber in Great Smoky
Mountains National
Park contain some of
the largest tulip poplar
trees in the eastern
United States.

6.6 miles to Cosby Campground. Greenbrier Cove is 15.9 miles to the right. Continue straight on the Maddron Bald Trail. The trail meanders through a second-growth tulip poplar forest at the base of Maddron Bald. Remnants of early house sites can be seen (stone fences and chimneys). A golden tulip poplar canopy covers the reds of maple and dogwood trees in autumn.

The old jeep road ends in a circle at 2.3 miles and becomes a foot trail. At that point, the forest takes on a different character with large trees towering over thick rhododendron. It's no wonder that early settlers called rhododendron thickets "hells." That's exactly what it's like to pass through them. The trail climbs steeply 0.3 miles to Indian Camp Creek, which offers a beautiful spot to rest or picnic. Enjoy the sound of the water in the cool shade.

A spring blizzard at Albright Grove.

The Albright Grove Trail begins at 2.9 miles and is marked with a sign. This trail is 0.7 miles and returns to the Maddron Bald Trail 0.3 miles above where it began, making the entire loop 1 mile long. Maddron Bald is to the right, after the upper junction of the Albright Grove Trail and the Maddron Bald Trail.

Since the area was never logged, this is truly an old-growth forest containing some of the largest tulip poplar trees in the park. It also has many species of other large trees. Some of the largest hemlocks have died in recent years due to the hemlock woolly adelgid. Some of these trees are 300–350 years old. Take a tape measure to record the circumference of these giants. It is a wonderful example of what the Smokies looked like before they were extensively logged in the beginning of the twentieth century.

This grove of old-growth forest, which lies between Indian Camp Creek and Dunn Creek, was named for Horace M. Albright, the second director of the National Park Service. Albright was the first assistant director of the Park Service while serving as superintendent of Yellowstone. He worked to help establish the Smokies as a national park during his tenure as director.

The grove is well worth the hike, especially in spring when wildflowers are an added attraction to this already beautiful spot. Since fewer people visit this area, the chance of seeing wildlife is better.

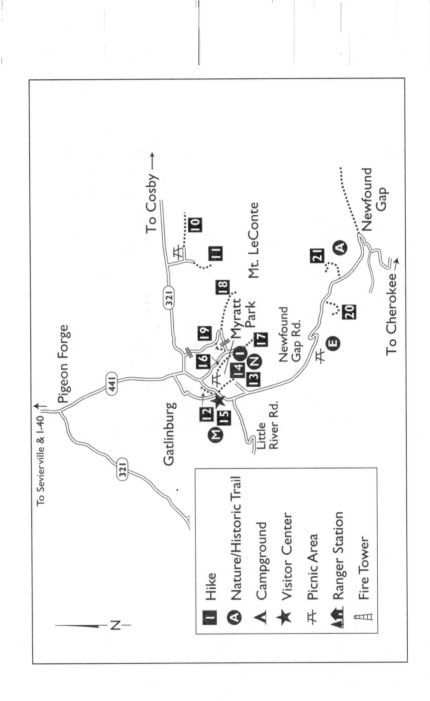

Gatlinburg–Mount LeConte

Gatlinburg is the northern gateway to the Smokies. It is a popular tourist spot with plenty of shops and attractions. The Gatlinburg Craftsman Loop is east of the town, off US 321 on the way to Cosby. The Sugarlands Visitor Center is next to park headquarters, 2 miles south of Gatlinburg on US 441. A museum, movie, and self-guided trail are part of the services available at the center.

Eastbound on I-40, take Exit 407 (TN 66) to Sevierville. Then follow US 441 through Pigeon Forge and Gatlinburg. Westbound on I-40, take Exit 443 onto the Foothills Parkway. At the end of the Foothills Parkway, turn left on US 321 and go to Gatlinburg via Cosby.

The bypass from Pigeon Forge to Sugarlands around Gatlinburg is a real time-saver during peak tourist season and has scenic overlooks of Gatlinburg and Mt. LeConte. From Cherokee, take the Newfound Gap Road (US 441) 30 miles north over the crest of the Smokies where you will cross the Appalachian Trail at Newfound Gap. This road may be closed in the winter due to snow and ice.

Mt. LeConte, one of the most popular hiking destinations in the Smokies, is the third highest peak (6,593 feet) in the park. It boasts excellent views from three points: Cliff Top, High Top, and Myrtle Point. A shelter, which sleeps 12, is often full and requires a reservation through the Park Backcountry Office. LeConte Lodge, established in 1925, provides food and lodging in a special setting. Advanced reservations can be made by calling (865) 429-5704; online at http://www.lecontelodge.com; or by email at reservations@lecontelodge. Usually reservations have to be made about one year in advance. Sunset from Cliff Top and sunrise from Myrtle Point are not to be missed.

Since it is difficult for children to make a day hike to the top and back, it is possible to walk lower sections. However, for the adventurous child, a hike to the summit of LeConte is a great accomplishment.

A major forest fire ravaged the Gatlinburg–Mt. LeConte area in November, 2016. The blaze began near the Chimney Tops and smoldered for a few days before spreading north through the park and into Gatlinburg, pushed by high winds and fueled by drought conditions. Nearly

2,000 structures were damaged or destroyed. No National Park Service buildings were lost in this fire, but damage in the forest will be visible for years to come. The Smokies, with a high annual rainfall, will recover quickly from this fire.

Gatlinburg can have heavy traffic, but don't let that keep you from wonderful hikes in this area.

10. RAMSEY CASCADES

8 miles roundtrip

Allow 5.5 to 7 hours

Elementary schoolers and **teens** will enjoy this moderate hike that gains 2,000 feet in 4 miles. This hike offers one of the highest waterfalls in the park, spring wildflowers, large trees, and beautiful streams.

How to Get There: From Gatlinburg, go east on US 321 toward Cosby. Turn into the Greenbrier entrance to the park, located 6 miles from traffic light #3 at the intersection of US 321 and US 441 in Gatlinburg. Follow the Middle Prong of the Little Pigeon River for 3.2 miles. Make a left turn over the wooden bridge. In 1.5 miles, the gravel road dead-ends at the trailhead. Pit toilets at the picnic area are the closest rest stops.

Description of the Hike: The first 1.5 miles of the trail is a pleasant walk on a gently graded gravel road with easy access to the Middle Prong of the Little Pigeon River. Benches provide an opportunity for a rest. After the parking area, the trail turns left and crosses a wooden bridge over Ramsey Branch. The trail passes through several large boulder fields, which were probably formed 10,000–12,000 years ago. At 1.5 miles, the old roadbed ends in a loop.

Continue straight ahead on the foot trail, which climbs gradually through rhododendron and dying hemlock. Notice the large hemlocks and tulip trees. At 2 miles, the trail descends to a large footlog, then turns left through some very large trees. Large silver bells and sweet birch trees are on the left and right sides of the trail, respectively. The tulip trees along this section of the trail are enormous! Try to hold hands and reach around them. The trail levels off for 0.25 miles before climbing again. At 2.7 miles, there is easy access to the creek, which is a good spot to rest before ascending again.

At 2.9 miles, after another footlog, the trail occasionally climbs rock steps as it approaches the cascades. Take extra care when crossing the stream because wet rocks can be slippery and unsteady. Ramsey Cascades tumbles 105 feet down a rocky wall. It is one of the highest cascades in the park and provides a great show in the wetter seasons of winter and spring. We've seen Ramsey Cascades completely frozen over in mid-February. About 100 feet below the cascades is a good place to cross the stream and take photographs.

The temptation to climb the rocks and boulders at the base and sides of the cascades is strong. This is *very dangerous*. Enjoy the view from the bottom, which is a good spot for a picnic. Return to the parking area by the same route.

Ramsey Cascades is a good hike any time of the year. Spring highlights include Clinton's lily, silver bell, and rhododendron, to name only a few. Summer is fun because the shady trail offers chances to play in the cool mountain stream. Fall and winter are also wonderful times to see the large trees. A light dusting of snow on one winter hike revealed the prints of many different types of animals and birds (but no humans). This trail is rarely crowded.

11. PORTERS CREEK AND FERN BRANCH FALLS

2. miles roundtrip to Smoky Mountain Hiking Club cabin

3.6 miles roundtrip to Fern Branch Falls

Allow 2 to 3 hours

Elementary schoolers will like these trips to an old cabin, a barn, and a waterfall. Historic rock walls, chimneys, and a cemetery are along the way.

How to Get There: The Porters Creek Trailhead is in the Greenbrier section of the park. The Greenbrier entrance to the park is approximately 6 miles east of Gatlinburg on US 321. After turning onto the Greenbrier road, travel straight for about 4 miles. The gravel road ends at a loop where parking is available.

Description of the Hike: Porters Creek Trail begins at a gate on a gravel road. Initially the trail climbs gently, but it quickly moderates for a very pleasant walk. Springtime offers abundant wildflowers on this first section of the trail as it follows Porters Creek through an area that was once farmed. The easy walk along the wide road travels through an area rich in cultural history.

About 0.5 miles into the walk, there is a nice bench for a rest. If smaller children are tiring, this makes a good turnaround point. Notice the old home sites and rock walls in this area. The trail crosses Long Branch on a bridge at about 0.7 miles. Just past the bridge, there are stone steps on the right that lead up to an old cemetery where Ownbys, Whaleys, and Profitts are buried.

The trail continues beside Porters Creek to a small branch crossing on a footlog. Just beyond the footlog, the gravel road ends at an old turnaround loop. This area is known as Porters Flats and is 1 mile from the trailhead.

The Brushy Mountain Trail and Smoky Mountain Hiking Club cabin are to the right. From this point, it is 4.5 miles to Trillium Gap via the Brushy Mountain Trail. Just a few yards along the Brushy Mountain Trail is a short spur trail that leads to the John Messer barn, built in 1875. Behind the barn, a path goes to a small branch where a springhouse still stands. Beyond the springhouse is the old Smoky Mountain Hiking Club cabin, built in 1934–1935. Exploring this area is interesting, but use caution when in and around the buildings. This can also be a good turnaround point, making the hike a 2-mile roundtrip.

Porters Creek Trail continues straight, past the loop, and becomes a typical hiking trail. Easy walking takes you above Porters Creek, on the left, and passes through an eastern hemlock forest that is under attack by the hemlock woolly adelgid. Some of these trees have been treated but others have died.

The Underworld
A Cherokee Legend

The Cherokee believed that a duplicate world existed beneath the ground. The only difference between the worlds was that the seasons were opposite. They saw proof of this in the springs that ran cool in the hot summer and warm in the freezing winter. Also, caves were warm during the coldest days and cool during the hottest times.

At 1.5 miles, cross Porters Creek on a footlog. The crossing is wider than most, and the creek is usually deep here; so use caution. On the other side of the creek, the forest floor becomes more open and is covered with wildflowers in springtime. Continue along the left side of Porters Creek for another 0.3 miles to Fern Branch Falls. The 45-foot cascade, to the left of the trail, is a pleasant and scenic spot. This is a good place to relax and enjoy the waterfall before making the 1.8-mile return to the parking area. This is a fun walk any time of year, but spring is magical with wildflowers.

12. GATLINBURG TRAIL

4 miles roundtrip

Allow 2 hours

Preschoolers and **elementary schoolers** will like this walk on a graveled pathway beside the West Prong of the Little Pigeon River. It is possible to take strollers on this walk.

How to Get There: From Gatlinburg, follow US 441 South into the park approximately 2 miles. Park at the Sugarlands Visitor Center.

Description of the Hike: This is an easy hike for all ages. Reminders of the past are alongside the trail. The present interrupts with sounds and sights of traffic on the highway. To begin, walk past the restrooms on the asphalt path into the woods, where you pass the Fighting Creek Nature Trail to the left. Proceed in front of the park headquarters building to the end of the asphalt path, where a sign directs you onto Park Headquarters Road. Turn left and walk a well-worn path on the side of this road for 0.3 miles to the park's maintenance area. Another sign points you to the trail, much of which follows the old road from Gatlinburg to Sugarlands as it parallels the West Prong of the Little Pigeon River.

At the beginning of the walk, look across the large island at the stone wall on the opposite side of the river. This wall is a result of clearing fields by moving the rocks to the river. Stroll through rhododendron and hardwoods to where the river reunites in a torrent, smoothing stones and undercutting the ledge on which you are standing.

At 0.5 miles, the trail passes under the Gatlinburg Bypass. This stretch is flat and pleasant with cool spots to play in the water. Climb a short incline away from the river to pass between chimneys and foundations of houses from another time. Descend into a flat area where second-growth poplar trees indicate that this area was probably farmed at one time.

The trail then turns right to cross the river on a steel and wooden bridge. The trail comes close to the busy highway and then recedes into the woods. Allow your children to linger and enjoy the river as you move toward Gatlinburg.

The trail returns once more to the highway before it divides into two short legs that both terminate at River Road in Gatlinburg. Return by the same trail. This trail can also be used to walk to the Sugarlands Visitor Center or Cataract Falls (see Hike #15 on page 32) from Gatlinburg. Cataract Falls is a nice side trip when walking to or from Gatlinburg. Take care to hold your children's hands when near the highway.

13. SUGARLANDS VALLEY

0.5 miles roundtrip

Allow 30 to 45 minutes

This is a wonderful short walk for **preschoolers**, featuring old house sites, creeks, exhibits, and bear footprints. A stroller or wheelchair can easily go on this all-access trail.

How to Get There: The trailhead is at a parking area 0.25 miles beyond the Sugarlands Visitor Center on the Newfound Gap Road (US 441).

Description of the Hike: This short trail is a loop beside the West Prong of the Little Pigeon River. Signs along the way tell of the human and natural history of the area. Go 75 yards from the parking lot on the trail. Turn left at the junction and walk toward the river. You will pass two chimneys that were once vacation homes in the Sugarlands community. Many people lived and farmed this area, but the two houses that stood on this site were mountain getaways, not permanent homes.

Sit on one of the benches to enjoy the sound of the river rushing over the rounded stones. Notice the footprints of a bear that wandered along one evening after the workmen left the cement to dry. We enjoy this short walk as a respite from the hustle and bustle of the busy highway.

14. OLD SUGARLANDS

3.4 miles roundtrip

Allow 3 hours

Elementary schoolers and **teens** will enjoy this moderate hike through an old Smoky Mountain community to the site of a Civilian Conservation Corps (CCC) camp.

How to Get There: The trailhead is at the north end (toward Gatlinburg) of the US 441 bridge over the West Prong of the Little Pigeon River. Park at the parking lot at Great Smoky Mountains National Park Headquarters or at the Sugarlands Visitor Center. Carefully cross the busy highway and then walk across the stone bridge. The Old Sugarlands Trailhead is on the right. (There is a pull-off that will accommodate a few cars at the trailhead, which can sometimes be difficult to access due to traffic.)

Description of the Hike: The trail begins on an old roadbed. After about 50 yards, the Twomile Branch Horse Trail veers off to the left. Continue to the right as you follow the old road. A rocky cliff is the site of an old quarry that supplied gravel for early paved road construction in the Smokies. This metamorphic sandstone is some of the oldest rock in the park. The rush of the West Prong of the Little Pigeon River drowns out the sound of the busy highway nearby.

At about 0.7 miles, the trail turns to the right off the old roadbed. Be careful, it can be confusing here because it looks like the trail should follow the roadbed up the ridge (this is the Grassy Branch Horse Trail). Step down to the right at the trail sign.

At 1 mile, cross over Bull Head Branch on an old bridge. Rotting telephone poles to the right of the trail are evidence that this section of the trail follows old TN 71, which was the first paved highway into the Smokies. The trail was also an early route before roads existed. This area was the center of the Sugarlands community named for the many sugar maples making up the forest. Notice the occasional piles of rock, indicating old house sites.

For a few hundred yards the trail runs along the right side of Bull Head Branch. Take a sharp left away from the river. Go a few hundred yards more to a T-junction where you will go to the right. In a few more feet, an indistinct trail to the left of the main trail leads to a CCC camp

CCC camp near Mt. Sterling P. O. Herbert M. Webster Photograph Collection, Betsey B. Creekmore Special Collections and University Archives, University of Tennessee, Knoxville Libraries.

The CCC

In the 1930s and early 1940s the United States was in the depths of the Great Depression with unemployment at an all-time high. President Franklin D. Roosevelt worked with Congress to create programs that would put people to work. The Civilian Conservation Corps (CCC), which began in 1933, put young men to work in America's national and state parks. Twenty-one CCC camps were built in the Smokies with numerous spike camps in remote areas. CCC boys built roads, bridges, buildings, fire towers, and trails—miles and miles of trails.

CCC men were paid $30 a month. They got to keep $5 each month, while $25 was sent home to help their families. Remnants of CCC camps can be seen all around the Smokies. Be grateful for the work that these young men of "Roosevelt's Army" did in the Smokies and other parks.

that stood here from 1933 to 1942. After the CCC was decommissioned, the camp was used to house conscientious objectors during World War II. Take time to explore the ruins of this old camp. Rock walls, foundations, and even the garbage dump offer clues to the life of this place that housed so many young men who helped to shape Great Smoky Mountains National Park.

Near the CCC camp, an old roadbed turns off to the right, leading to the Sugarlands Community Cemetery about 0.3 miles away. It is an interesting place; just remember that this side trip will add 0.6 miles to your walk. You can continue up the old roadbed, the Old Sugarlands Trail, another 2.2 miles to Cherokee Orchard above Gatlinburg. This climb up the ridge gains about 900 feet. We usually enjoy this walk to the CCC camp, then turn around and return by the same route for a nice 3.4-mile walk. In the spring, wildflowers abound, while the fall has a beautiful display of leaves. This is a walk back in time to the early years of the park.

15. CATARACT FALLS

1 mile roundtrip

Allow 1 hour

Preschoolers and older adults can make this easy stroll to a nice waterfall.

How to Get There: Begin at the Sugarlands Visitor Center outside Gatlinburg.

Description of the Hike: Go about 75 yards past the restrooms toward the headquarters building. Turn left onto the Fighting Creek Nature Trail, and follow the nature trail about 0.2 miles. Cross Fighting Creek on a foot bridge, then turn right and walk beside the flowing waters of Fighting Creek. There are some nice spots for creek play.

The trail passes under a road bridge behind park headquarters. On the other side of the bridge, climb the few steps to the left to an old roadbed just to the right of the paved road. Turn right and walk about 225 yards beside Fighting Creek to Cataract Falls.

For a shorter version of this walk for short legs, simply park in the lot at the end of the bridge behind park headquarters. Cross the bridge, turn right onto the trail, and walk for about 225 yards to the falls.

Cataract Falls is a nice cascade that slides down a rocky metasandstone face. At the bottom, Cataract Branch joins Fighting Creek. The word cataract is from the Latin word *cataracta* meaning "waterfall." So the name means Waterfall Falls. This is a small waterfall (about 40 feet), which is a nice complement to the Fighting Creek Nature Trail and the Sugarlands Visitor Center or the Gatlinburg Trail.

16. TWIN CREEKS

4.4 miles roundtrip

Allow 2 to 3 hours

Elementary schoolers will enjoy this walk through old house sites and rock walls, passing the Twin Creeks Science and Education Center to the Noah "Bud" Ogle place.

How to Get There: On US 441 in Gatlinburg, turn onto Airport Road/ Historic Nature Trail Road and drive about 0.75 miles to Mynatt Park on the right. Mynatt Park is a City of Gatlinburg park that was once a Methodist church camp. Park in the lot at Mynatt Park. Walk out to the main road, turn right, and walk into Great Smoky Mountains National Park. The trailhead is on the right just past the park entrance sign.

Description of the Hike: This trail climbs gradually through mountain vacation house sites, old farm sites, and a recovering forest. Begin to the right of the park road on an old roadbed. A chimney from a vacation home is off to the left. Follow the trail about 700 yards to a small footlog that crosses Watercrease Branch. Just after the creek crossing, Grassy Branch Horse Trail comes in from the right.

The trail meanders past rock walls and rock piles as well as through a second-growth forest that was once fields. LeConte Creek, which tumbles off the steep slopes of Mt. LeConte, flows to the right of the trail. At 1.2 miles, the trail crosses a paved road and an old stone wall at the Twin Creeks Science and Education Center. The park's science research has been headquartered in this area for decades. The Twin Creeks Center was built in the early 2000s.

Continue uphill about 400 yards to rock hop across a tributary of LeConte Creek. The area gets its name from the "twin" creeks that form LeConte Creek. Notice more rock walls and rock piles. At 1.9 miles from the beginning, the trail dead-ends into the Noah "Bud" Ogle Nature Trail. Turn left and walk 0.3 miles to the Noah "Bud" Ogle homesite. (See Appendix 1, page 110 for information on the Noah "Bud" Ogle Nature Trail.)

For a 4.4-mile-roundtrip walk, simply turn around and walk back down to Mynatt Park. The main road is only 100 yards or so from the trail. Or, this walk can be started at the other end, if you would rather park at the Ogle place. Two cars, one at each end, makes this a 2.2-mile walk. The nature trail is about 1 mile long and a great place to explore the Smokies very close to downtown Gatlinburg.

17. RAINBOW FALLS

5.5 miles roundtrip

Allow 3 to 4 hours

Older elementary schoolers and **teens** will be challenged by this moderate hike to a waterfall on the side of Mt. LeConte. This hike offers spring wildflowers, fall colors, a waterfall, and a creek.

How to Get There: On US 441 in Gatlinburg, turn onto Airport Road/Historic Nature Trail Road at traffic light #8. It is 3.4 miles to the Rainbow Falls/Bullhead parking area. (You will pass the Noah "Bud" Ogle Nature Trail on the right, 2.6 miles from downtown Gatlinburg.) Rainbow Falls is a very popular trail, and the parking lot can often be overcrowded.

Description of the Hike: This multiple-use trail goes 2.7 miles to Rainbow Falls on its way to the top of Mt. LeConte (6.7 miles). The trail follows LeConte Creek up to the falls. One is never far from the sound of the mountain stream that falls from high up the slopes of Mt. LeConte toward its union with the West Prong of the Little Pigeon River in Gatlinburg. This creek was once known as Mill Creek because it had 14 tub mills similar to the one at the Noah "Bud" Ogle place.

Just over 1 mile up the trail, a switchback provides an overlook with a good view of Sevier County. Some fire damage from the 2016 fire is visible in this area. When the creek comes back into view, make the first of two creek crossings on a footlog. In 0.5 miles cross another smaller creek at the base of a small 10-foot waterfall. The second crossing is over a bridge of several large stones. Many large hemlocks and rhododendron thickets border the creeks. In the spring, trillium and violets crowd the trail. The falls is in view just upstream. Near the base of the 75-foot falls is a third crossing of LeConte Creek on a large slab of stone quarried nearby. The afternoon sun can produce a rainbow effect (thus the name) as the creek plunges over the cliff.

In the winter, ice from the spray transforms the trail, rock, and creek crossings into beautiful but dangerous sights. Rainbow Falls is a nice, cool spot at the end of a summer hike or a way station on the route to the top of Mt. LeConte. Spring wildflowers are plentiful; while fall shows a totally different set of colors. Remember that water flow depends on rainfall, so the waterfall can be a trickle or a torrent. The top of Mt. LeConte is about 4 miles beyond Rainbow Falls.

This trail was reconstructed and rebuilt in 2018 through the Friends of the Smokies' Trails Forever program. The improvements to creek crossings, steps, and wet areas have transformed this well-traveled trail into a delight to walk.

18. GROTTO FALLS AND BRUSHY MOUNTAIN

2.6 miles or 6.8 miles roundtrip

Allow 3 or 6 hours

The first part of the hike, to Grotto Falls, is good for **preschoolers** and **elementary schoolers**. It rises only 500 feet in elevation over 1.5 miles. This walk offers a beautiful waterfall, spring wildflowers, and fall colors. Beyond Grotto Falls, **older elementary schoolers** and **teens** will be challenged on the climb to Trillium Gap and Brushy Mountain. This is the trail used by the llamas that supply LeConte Lodge three times a week. It is a very popular trail, and the parking lot can often be overcrowded.

How to Get There: From Gatlinburg's main street (US 441), turn onto Airport Road/Historic Nature Trail Road at traffic light #8. At 2.6 miles from the light, pass the Noah "Bud" Ogle Nature Trail. Beyond the Ogle place, where the road divides, take the right fork, which goes through second-growth forest. Look for rock piles left by farmers who cleared the land. At 3.4 miles, pass the Rainbow Falls–Bullhead trailheads that lead to Mt. LeConte. At 3.7 miles, turn right onto the *one-way* Roaring Fork Motor Nature Trail (booklet at the gate). (NOTE: The Roaring Fork Motor Nature Trail is closed in the winter.) Two miles from the gate along the auto trail (5.7 miles from Gatlinburg), the Grotto Falls Trail begins on the right, beyond the parking lot. A portable toilet is available at the parking area.

Description of the Hike: This easy trail lends itself to walking side by side. It begins in a hemlock forest but gives way to tulip trees and yellow buckeye. On the climb from the road toward the creek, more rhododendrons are found. An abundance of mountain laurel and fern is also present. Small streams have to be crossed but pose no problem except in the rainy seasons. Trillium, violets, and spring beauty are plentiful in late April and early May.

After reaching the falls, it is fun to walk on the trail behind the waterfall, the easiest way to get to the other side. The pool at the foot of the falls is a favorite spot to cool hot feet. In the spring and fall many salamanders can be seen. The falls, which are about 25 feet high, have a pretty good flow even in the drier seasons. Roaring Fork Creek is said to be one of the steepest creeks in the east. It loses 1 mile in elevation from its source near the top of Mt. LeConte to its mouth in Gatlinburg.

Red squirrels and deer are often seen in this area. Spring, summer, and fall are all wonderful times to visit this easily accessible spot. In the winter, the Roaring Fork Motor Nature Trail is closed. The falls can be reached, but the roundtrip hike is 4 miles longer.

From Grotto Falls, it is another 1.7 miles to Trillium Gap and an additional 0.4 miles to the crest of Brushy Mountain. The trail becomes considerably steeper after leaving the falls, but if you have the time and energy, walking this section in springtime is well worth the effort. Trillium, squirrel corn, and spring beauty abound all along the trail. Trillium Gap provides a special show in late April to early May. The show varies from season to season, but this gap is usually carpeted with spring beauty, sprinkled with trout lilies and trillium. This is a great place to relax and enjoy a break. This area looks like a crossroads of Trillium Gap

Ka'lanu, The Raven

As a young man growing up in the frontier town of Maryville, Sam Houston went to live among the Cherokee. He was adopted by Chief Jolly and given the name *Ka'lanu*, the Raven. He fought in the Battle of Horseshoe Bend with Andrew Jackson and the Cherokee against the Creek Indians.

Houston was a friend to the Cherokee throughout his political career. He served as a member of the US House of Representatives, as a US Senator, as Governor of Tennessee, as President of the Republic of Texas, and as Governor of Texas. He is one of the few men to have served as governor of two states. A schoolhouse in which he taught still stands near Maryville.

Trail and Brushy Mountain Trail, but the two trails meet only briefly before diverging again. As you reach the gap from Grotto Falls, you will see Brushy Mountain Trail entering the gap straight ahead of you. It turns to your left for another 0.4 miles to the crest of Brushy Mountain, while Trillium Gap Trail goes right for another 3.6 miles to Mt. LeConte. The trails never cross, just share a few feet of common ground.

Leave Trillium Gap by turning left onto the Brushy Mountain Trail. The 0.4-mile walk is not very steep but can be difficult in places. The larger trees quickly give way to a narrow rut of a trail through a rhododendron and laurel tunnel, which can be muddy with lots of roots to trip you up. After the tunnel, the trail opens into a heath bald, which is especially nice with blooming plants in spring and early summer. Galax, trailing arbutus, and wintergreen grow along the trail, while sand myrtle, huckleberry, and blueberries cover the bald, along with other heath plants. Views of fall colors are wonderful. Walking around the bald can provide limited views. To the northeast is Greenbrier Pinnacle, and to the south, the massive Mt. LeConte rises high above Trillium Gap. There are some nice spots to enjoy a break or lunch before starting back. The return trip of 3.4 miles is an easy walk, and you may find that you enjoy different highlights on the way down.

Do not be tempted to leave your pack at Trillium Gap for the walk out to Brushy Mountain. We have seen some hikers do this, and it can be a *very dangerous* situation. Bears frequent this gap for the tender spring plants, fall beechnuts, or a *careless* hiker's pack. This trail can be very crowded, especially during summer.

19. BASKINS CREEK FALLS

3 or 3.4 miles roundtrip

Allow 4 hours

Elementary schoolers and older children will like this moderate hike past old house sites to a 35-foot waterfall. This is a nice hike that is easily made from two different directions. Both are about the same distance and difficulty.

How to Get There: ALTERNATE ONE: From Gatlinburg's main street (US 441), turn onto Airport Road/Historic Nature Trail Road at traffic light #8. At 2.6 miles from the light, pass the Noah "Bud" Ogle Nature Trail. Beyond the Ogle place, where the road divides, take the right fork

of Cherokee Orchard Road. At 3.4 miles, pass the Rainbow Falls–Bullhead parking area, where pit toilets are available. At 3.7 miles, turn right
onto the *one-way* Roaring Fork Motor Nature Trail (booklet available for
a small fee at the gate). (NOTE: The Roaring Fork Motor Nature Trail is
closed in the winter.) About 0.2 miles from the gate is limited pull-off
parking on either side of the road and a sign on the left marking the
Baskins Creek Trail. There is a parking lot located on the right side of
the road, just before reaching the gate to Roaring Fork Motor Nature
Trail. This is the only place to park in the winter and the best place to
park anytime. You can walk up the road 0.2 miles, but the best way to
reach the trailhead is on an unmarked trail starting at the upper end of
the parking lot. The trail parallels the road to intersect with the Trillium Gap Trail, turns left, and after several yards, reaches the road and
Baskins Creek Trail. While walking up this short connecter trail, look
around to notice the wide terraces in the second-growth tulip trees; this
is where the Cherokee Orchard fruit trees once grew. Keep in mind that
this parking lot will add 0.4 miles to your roundtrip but will allow you to

Waterfalls, like Baskins
Creek Falls, are a wonderful place for children to
experience the miracle of
the Smokies.

return to Gatlinburg without driving around the one-way motor nature trail, if so desired.

Description of the Hike: Leaving the road, the Baskins Creek Trail crosses an open forest to an easy ascent of a ridge. This area burned heavily in the Gatlinburg fire of November, 2016. The trail follows the ridge crest for a short distance through a dry pine forest and mountain laurel. As the trail descends the ridge, the forest becomes primarily oak

Peregrine Falcon

The peregrine falcon is an amazing bird of prey that feeds on other birds. The falcon takes birds in mid-air with a dive that can be faster than 180 miles per hour! Falcons' homes (called eyries) are built on cliffs and ledges. The park was home to many falcons until the 1940s when they quit nesting in the Smokies.

In 1997, the peregrine falcon returned to Little Duck Hawk Ridge after an absence of about 50 years. Like many other birds of prey, the peregrine falcon was pushed to the brink of extinction because of human use of DDT. With the ban on DDT and ongoing recovery efforts, most birds of prey have made a comeback.

Over a three-year period in the mid-1980s, 13 peregrine falcon chicks were "hacked" (given partial freedom to learn to fly and hunt before being released) in the park. Although there is no way to know for certain, the return of the peregrine is probably a result of the recovery efforts there. The adult pair that returned in 1997 had three offspring that fledged successfully that year, as well as several other successful nestings. In 2007, no nest was recorded at Little Duck Hawk Ridge. Peregrine falcons have been seen on Greenbrier Pinnacle over several years. It is strongly suspected that they are nesting there, but at the time of this writing, that has not been confirmed. To learn more about peregrine falcons, go to https://www.birds.cornell.edu/.

with galax along the trail. About 1 mile from the trailhead, you will reach an easy crossing of Falls Branch before the trail descends more steeply. After a short descent through a canyon, the area becomes more open. You will see a sign on the left marking a side trail to Baskins Cemetery. It is 300 yards up the ridge to the cemetery after easy crossings of Falls Branch. This is typical of community cemeteries found in several areas of the Smokies. Past the cemetery sign, the trail continues beside Falls Branch to another sign at 1.4 miles from the trailhead. The sign indicates the mileage—1.4 miles to Trillium Gap Trail (back the way you came) and 1.3 miles to Roaring Fork Road straight ahead. At this sign is an additional side trail that leads to Baskins Creek Falls. Turn left on the side trail and walk the 500 yards to the falls. You will immediately pass an old home site on the right and cross an area that was once farmed. The last 100 yards down to the falls is steep and rocky.

The waters of Falls Branch do a two-step off a metasandstone ledge to drop 35 feet onto the rocks below. The cliffs show several interesting geological features. To the left of the falls, vertical fractures known as joints can be seen in the Roaring Fork Sandstone. A layering effect can best be seen to the right of the falls.

To the right of the falls, about 100 feet up the ridge, is a wet-weather falls. We've noticed dirt daubers' nests stuck to the side of the cliff. The mud is from the creek below.

Help children to see that the landscape is being formed and is still in transition. Point out the large boulder at the base of the falls. From where might it have fallen? Perhaps it was pushed out of the cliff at the very spot where the creek now pours.

Baskins Creek, just downstream from the falls, gets its name from a man called Bearskin Joe who lived nearby and was known as a great hunter, especially of bear. The creek was called Bearskin Joe's Creek, which later became Bearskin Creek. This name was eventually misunderstood and shortened to Baskins Creek. Climb the trail back up to the house site and the main trail, then return to the trailhead by the same route.

How to Get There: ALTERNATE TWO: Follow the above directions to the Roaring Fork Motor Nature Trail, continuing through the gate. Pass the Grotto Falls parking area at 2 miles (5.7 miles from downtown Gatlinburg) to a parking area 3 miles from the gate (6.7 miles from Gatlinburg). This parking area is on the left before the road crosses Roaring Fork. A sign for a cemetery stands at the edge of the parking lot. The nearest restrooms are pit toilets at the Rainbow Falls parking area.

Description of the Hike: Walk on the Baskins Creek Trail to the cemetery, which was restored in 1991. Many of the graves are of the Bales and Ogle families. The house across the creek from the parking area was the Jim Bales place. His family and his brother, Ephraim, lived in the immediate area. One of those buried in the cemetery was supposedly the first child born in what is now Gatlinburg. Notice the dates on the tombstones that serve as reminders of the difficult lives of previous inhabitants.

The trail continues past the graveyard over a ridge of pine and mountain laurel. A long descent on the other side follows an old mountain road through a hemlock forest with a thick rhododendron understory. This is particularly beautiful in June when the rhododendrons are in bloom. The trail reaches a creek and moderates considerably. Notice the quartz scattered along the trail in this section. Follow the creek for about 200 yards before turning left to cross it and ascend a ridge. After climbing the ridge, you reach an open area that was once a farm. Here you will see a sign marking the mileage—1.4 miles to Trillium Gap Trail and 1.3 miles to Roaring Fork Road. From here the hike to Baskins Creek Falls is the same as described above for the Alternate One hike.

A nice side trip that will extend this walk only 0.75 miles is to Baskins Cemetery and Falls Branch. After returning to the trail junction from the falls, turn right. A sign points to the side trail up the ridge to the small Baskins Cemetery. Most of the tombstones have no writing, but a few tell of deaths around the beginning of the twentieth century.

Return to the main trail and continue right just a little farther to observe Falls Branch tripping and trickling off Piney Mountain. The branch is not wide but makes a long, thin cascade beside the trail for nearly 0.25 miles.

Return to your car by the same route.

20. CHIMNEY TOPS

3.5 miles roundtrip

Allow 4 to 5 hours

Older elementary schoolers and **teens** will be fascinated by the view from the viewing platform at the end of this strenuous hike, which gains 1,350 feet in 1.75 miles. This hike offers views, a creek, and spring wildflowers.

How to Get There: Follow Newfound Gap Road (US 441) 7 miles from the Sugarlands Visitor Center at Gatlinburg to a parking area beyond the tunnel. Do not confuse the Chimney Tops Trailhead with the Chimneys Picnic Area (5 miles from the visitor center). The closest restrooms are at the Chimneys Picnic Area (2 miles from the trailhead) and at Newfound Gap (7 miles from the trailhead). From Cherokee, it is 22 miles from the Oconaluftee Visitor Center along Newfound Gap Road (US 441) to the trailhead.

Description of the Hike: Descend from the parking lot to cross the West Prong of the Little Pigeon River on a footbridge. The large boulders and rocks are part of the Thunderhead Formation of metamorphic sandstone that was formed 570 million years ago. A second footbridge crosses Road Prong, which flows into the West Prong of the Little Pigeon below the bridge.

The trail divides after the second bridge with the right fork going down to the Chimneys Picnic Area. Take the left fork, which ascends into rhododendron and hemlock. A third footbridge recrosses Road Prong 0.25 miles from the parking area. A gradual climb through an open area of second-growth forest, called Beech Flats, features many spring

Chimneys from New Found Gap Highway, 1933. Albert "Dutch" Roth Photograph Collection, Betsey B. Creekmore Special Collections and University Archives, University of Tennessee, Knoxille Libraries.

wildflowers, especially spring beauty and fringed phacelia. Cross the creek one last time at 0.75 miles, after which the trail divides again.

The trail to the left is the Road Prong Trail, which ascends 3.3 miles along Road Prong to the Appalachian Trail and Clingmans Dome Road at Indian Gap. The Road Prong Trail follows the route of one of the few roads over the crest of the Smokies until the modern highway was built. Settlers built the road along the route of a Cherokee footpath that crossed the Smokies for thousands of years. Cherokee Confederate troops completed the transmountain road during the Civil War. The Road Prong Trail is a beautiful hike for waterfalls and wildflowers but is best descended rather than ascended.

The trail to the Chimneys goes to the right. Rest here because the trail becomes *very* steep. Halfway up the steepest part, along many, many steps, is a pretty cascade. A switchback signals the end of the steepest section, but the climb continues, though it moderates. Walk the narrow ridgetop amid the tenacious grip of thousands of roots. At the end of the trail is a platform where you can see the Chimneys rise like a stone wall.

This trail was rebuilt in 2015 through the Friends of the Smokies' Trails Forever Program. The Gatlinburg fire in November, 2016, began on the slopes of Chimney Tops. The area was heavily burned. After the fire, the trail was rehabilitated and restored with the addition of the platform at the top; but the rocks and ground remain unstable and hiking is prohibited.

The stone of the Chimney Tops is the metamorphic Anakeesta rock formation. The view from the platform affords sights of the Chimneys and the higher Smokies. Mt. Mingus is to the southeast and Mt. LeConte to the northeast. Take plenty of water for this hike. The trail *ends* at the viewing platform! There is a large metal gate blocking the trail about 200 feet beyond the platform. *No one* should be anywhere near the natural chimneys! Return to the parking lot by the same route.

21. ALUM CAVE AND ARCH ROCK
TO MOUNT LECONTE

11 miles roundtrip

Allow 8 to 9 hours

Teens will find this difficult hike to the summit of LeConte rewarding. Younger children will enjoy the lower stretches of the hike to Arch Rock, Inspiration Point, and Alum Cave Bluffs.

How to Get There: The trailhead is located 8.6 miles from the Sugarlands Visitor Center, on Newfound Gap Road. It is approximately 20 miles from the Oconaluftee Visitor Center. There are two large parking areas, and a sign marks the trailhead. This is a very popular trail, and the parking lots can often be overcrowded. There are pit toilets in the lower parking area.

Description of the Hike: Alum Cave Trail is one of the most popular trails in the park and is the most traveled route to the summit of Mt. Le-Conte. Several points of interest are attractive well before reaching the summit and provide several options for hikers of all ages.

The trail starts near the junction of Walker Camp Prong and Alum Cave Creek. Within 200 yards after crossing Walker Camp Prong on a bridge, you will reach another bridge providing an easy crossing of Alum Cave Creek. Alum Cave Creek parallels the trail for about 1 mile before the steepest parts of the trail are encountered. Even the youngest children can enjoy this pleasant walk along the creek among rhododendron under large eastern hemlock trees. Many of these hemlock giants have succumbed to the hemlock woolly adelgid. Easy access to the creek, in several places, provides enjoyable spots for picnicking or just playing. Smaller children can have a rewarding hike by exploring this area and returning to the car at any point.

After meandering beside Alum Cave Creek for 1.1 miles, the trail then roughly follows Styx Branch for about 0.5 miles. Over the next 0.5 miles, the trail ascends through a predominantly yellow-birch forest and crosses Styx Branch four times on footlogs. At 1.4 miles, you cross the third footlog and enter Arch Rock. The rock that makes up Arch Rock is known as Anakeesta Formation, which comprises most of the structures in this area, including Inspiration Point, Alum Cave Bluffs, and Little Duck Hawk Ridge. Stone steps lead through the arch, which has a cable handhold to assist in the steep climb. As you climb, notice the roof of the arch and the sharp edges of the rock. Watch your head! Arch Rock was formed by a freezing and thawing process as opposed to the usual wearing away by water, which creates smooth stone surfaces. Arch Rock makes a good turnaround point for those who are only up for a 2.8-mile roundtrip hike.

Above Arch Rock, you cross the fourth footlog, then within a few hundred yards, you will encounter a washed-out section of Styx Branch. In 1993, a thunderstorm hung on the shoulders of Mt. LeConte, dropping a large amount of rain in a short amount of time. As a result, a wall of water and debris came roaring down the mountain deeply scarring this area. To your left, notice remnants of the log jam that caused the damaged stream bed that you are crossing. This has recovered well in the ensuing years. Although it is overgrown now, notice that the trees are smaller compared to the surrounding forest. After this crossing, the trail leaves the drainage areas and begins a steeper climb for approximately 0.5 miles.

At 2 miles, you reach Inspiration Point, a rocky spur consisting of the same Anakeesta Formation you saw at Arch Rock. This is a favorite resting spot for hikers because of the great views and pleasant surroundings. In mid-to-late summer, this heath bald is awash with color. Catawba rhododendron, sand myrtle, and other flowering shrubs cover this and surrounding ridges, providing a wonderful array of nature in bloom. Across the chasm to the right, Little Duck Hawk Ridge protrudes from the mountain into the valley below. Look closely at the ridge to see a hole in the rock, which was formed in the same way as Arch Rock. Just beyond and slightly higher than Little Duck Hawk Ridge, Big Duck Hawk Ridge can be seen. These parallel ridges were named for the peregrine falcons that nest here once again. At one time, the peregrine falcon was commonly called a "duck hawk."

The trail reaches Alum Cave Bluffs at 2.3 miles. These massive overhanging bluffs create a unique environment unlike any other area of the Smokies. The dry, powder-like dust contains several minerals, some very rare and others found nowhere else in the world. In the early 1900s, evidence of early mining efforts could still be found here. Limited mining

Smoky Jack

Smoky Jack was a German shepherd that had been trained as a police dog. He was first called Cumberland Jack, but when Paul Adams bought him, he became known as Smoky Jack. In 1925, Paul Adams established LeConte Lodge high atop Mt. LeConte (the third highest peak in the Smokies at 5,593 feet). Adams and Jack would walk down to Charlie Ogle's store in Gatlinburg and carry supplies back to the top of the mountain. Adams made packs that fit Jack so that he could carry 25 pounds of supplies. The story is that Adams would put lists for supplies in the packs and send Smoky Jack down to Charlie Ogle who would fill the order and send Jack back up the mountain.

for sulfides and saltpeter (both used to make gunpowder) took place here during the Civil War. Little is known about the extent of the mining that took place.

Leaving the bluffs, the trail climbs rather steeply to Gracies Pulpit. This rocky area is an approximate halfway point to the summit. It is named for Gracie McNichol who hiked to Mt. LeConte many times, even into her nineties. This is a good place to take a break and to enjoy views of LeConte across the valley. The trail descends for about 0.5 miles before starting to climb again. Passing through red spruce, yellow birch, and rhododendron, you will come to a switchback with stairs at 3.8 miles. From this point, it will be a steady climb for the next 1 mile. You will pass in and out of forest and open grassy areas where scars from past landslides are obvious. Mountain gentian and mountain krigia can be seen blooming in the grassy areas during the summer months. In this section, there are rocky and exposed places where cables have been installed along the trail for handholds. The rock can be wet in all seasons but can be icy in winter months, so use caution.

About 0.3 miles from the LeConte Lodge, you will walk under Cliff Top and reach a saddle between Cliff Top and West Point. The trail becomes almost flat at this point as you walk through a dying/regenerating forest of Fraser fir. At 5 miles, the trail intersects with the Rainbow Falls Trail, about 0.1 miles from Mt. LeConte Lodge. Continuing on the Rainbow Falls Trail, you will come to the side trail to Cliff Top on the right;

Smoky Jack with Saddle pockets, winter of 1932. Paul J. Adams Photograph Collection, University of Tennessee, Knoxville Libraries.

this trail leads 0.2 miles to wonderful views and a great place for lunch. Cliff Top is a must-see if you make the trip to LeConte.

To the left of the Cliff Top Trail are wide steps leading down to the lodge. While on top, you should visit the LeConte Lodge office to sign the register and check out the souvenirs that can only be bought there. Snacks are also available for a fee. LeConte Lodge was begun in 1925 and has been in operation ever since. To make reservations for an overnight stay, call 865-429-5704 or go online to http://www.lecontelodge.com.

If you have the time and energy, two other points of interest are enjoyable while on the summit. Return to the main trail via the steps, turn left at the top of the steps, and go approximately 0.3 miles on the Boulevard Trail to High Top, the highest point on Mt. LeConte at 6,593 feet above sea level. Another 0.25 miles down the Boulevard Trail is a side trail to the right, leading 0.2 miles to Myrtle Point. On a clear day, the views from Myrtle Point are incredible. You can see the main spine of the Smokies, Newfound Gap, and points beyond. The roundtrip from the lodge to Myrtle Point is about 1.5 miles, so plan your time wisely if you add this section to your hike.

A right turn at the top of the steps from the lodge will take you down Rainbow Falls Trail 0.1 mile to join Alum Cave Trail and the return trip to the trailhead. The 5-mile trip down Alum Cave Trail affords different views and can be more enjoyable than the strenuous trip up. Many enjoy this hike in all seasons. This trail can have dangerous sections of ice during the winter months. Use caution and consider some type of traction devices for your boots. As with any hike, remember to allow plenty of time, take proper clothing, food, and water. This can be a long but rewarding experience on the third highest peak in the Smokies.

The Alum Cave Trail is a beneficiary of the Trails Forever Program of the Friends of the Smokies. Two years of extensive work by the trail crew was required to rehabilitate and restore this very popular trail. A walk of any length is fun on this trail. Just remember that your child might tire before the destination is reached. It is best to have a great time with your child instead of pressing to an objective that might be beyond the child's abilities. Ask yourself—when was the last time you and your child walked one mile? two miles? or more? Creek play can be a most memorable moment.

Elkmont–Metcalf Bottoms

In the early years of the twentieth century, the Little River Logging Company of Townsend built a logging railroad from Townsend into the Smokies, following the Little River. As the area was cleared, the logging company ran "excursion" cars with the lumber cars on the train. Visitors came to play along the upper reaches of the Little River and its tributaries. By 1910 the lumber company sold lots to Knoxville citizens, who formed the Appalachian Club. They built a clubhouse and many summer homes. Soon after, the Wonderland Club, downstream from the Appalachian Club, built the Wonderland Hotel resort.

The two communities attracted many well-to-do people from all over Tennessee. Governor Austin Peay and Colonel David Chapman were among the many famous people who had vacation homes in the mountains at Elkmont. Many of these people worked to form Great Smoky Mountains National Park and were granted lifetime leases. After the leases were renewed several times, the National Park Service allowed them to run out at the end of 1992. Much controversy has centered on the fate of the old buildings. Look at these as you enter and leave but heed the keep-out signs. The buildings are old and not in good repair.

Elkmont is off the Little River Road between Gatlinburg and Townsend, 5 miles from Sugarlands Visitor Center toward Townsend and Cades Cove—or 13 miles from the Townsend Y (intersection of Townsend Road, Laurel Creek Road, and Little River Road) toward Gatlinburg. Elkmont is the place to watch the synchronous firefly display each June. For more information on this rare event, go to https://www .nps.gov/grsm/learn/nature/fireflies.htm.

The Metcalf Bottoms Picnic Area is 9.5 miles from Sugarlands Visitor Center and 9.3 miles from the Townsend Y. This is a very popular picnic spot along the shores of the Little River. It is a great place to access Curry Mountain, Little Greenbrier, and the Walker Sisters' homesite.

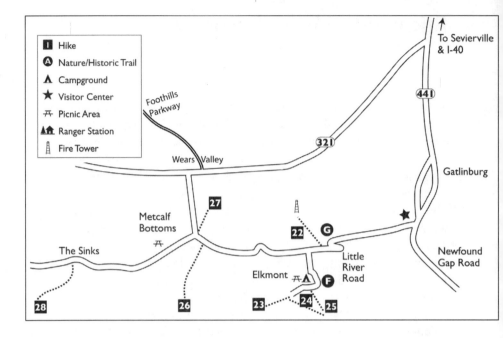

22. LAUREL FALLS–COVE MOUNTAIN FIRE TOWER

2.6 miles roundtrip—Allow 2 hours

8 miles roundtrip—Allow 5 to 5.5 hours

Preschoolers could go to Laurel Falls and back. However, **elementary schoolers** and **teens** would enjoy the moderate hike to the tower. This trail offers a waterfall, fire tower, wonderful views, and old-growth forest.

How to Get There: The trailhead is at Fighting Creek Gap along the Little River Road between Sugarlands and Townsend. Parking is available 3.8 miles from Sugarlands Visitor Center and 14 miles from the Townsend Y. The closest restrooms are at Elkmont Campground, 2 miles from Fighting Creek Gap (toward Townsend), or at the Sugarlands Visitor Center. This is a very popular spot and is often overcrowded. Start early in the morning or come in the off-season.

Description of the Hike: The first 1.3 miles is a paved, self-guided trail to Laurel Falls. A leaflet that describes interesting features on the way to Laurel Falls can be obtained, for a small charge, in a box at the trailhead.

The trail climbs through oak and hemlock with views of Meigs and Blanket Mountains to the southwest. In mid-May the mountain laurel blooms abundantly for a wonderful show of white and pink. This portion of the trail is easy and well suited for any age.

You will pass steep cliffs above and below the trail on the way to the falls, but there is no danger if everyone stays on the trail. Hold onto small hands so that no one strays too far. However, at other spots it is safe for children to be the leaders. Laurel Branch tumbles over cliffs of metasandstone to form beautiful falls through which the trail passes. This lovely spot is a popular site and can often be crowded. With younger children, it is best to turn around at Laurel Falls for a good 2.6-mile hike.

The stretch from the falls to the tower is definitely worth the effort; however, it is more difficult than the paved trail to Laurel Falls. We recommend it for older children and teens. To reach Cove Mountain and the fire tower, cross Laurel Branch on the concrete bridge and continue up the trail. The first mile steadily climbs Chinquapin Ridge through pine and laurel mixed with hardwood. One mile beyond the falls, the trail enters an old-growth forest of hemlocks and tulip trees. These large trees are magnificent! Children enjoy circling and photographing these old giants. Talk to your children about how trees grow, adding a tree ring each year. Why did these escape the logger's ax?

On top of Chinquapin Ridge, at 3.1 miles, the Little Greenbrier Trail goes left 4 miles to Wear Cove Gap. In spring time, galax, rhododendron, and mountain laurel bloom beside the trail. Continue ahead 0.9 miles to the fire tower. The first half of the last mile is easy with a slight descent. The last half mile climbs Cove Mountain. The trail comes to Cove Mountain Trail, running east and west, at 0.1 miles from the fire tower; Sugarlands Visitor Center is 9 miles to the right. The fire tower is to the left with a grassy area and large stones at its base.

The fire tower is one of only five remaining in the park. The Cove Mountain tower was built in 1935 and is 60 feet tall. Fire towers were an important part of protecting the national park and surrounding lands from devastating forest fires, but they are not used anymore because using airplanes is more economical and accurate. The steel tower is now used as an air-quality monitoring station, one of three monitoring stations in the park (the others being on Look Rock and Clingmans Dome).

Wear Cove, the Bluff Mountain section of Chilhowee Mountain, and Knoxville are to the north, with Cades Cove and Rich Mountain to the west. Be sure to take binoculars and a camera on this scenic hike. It is an easy return along the same route. Spring wildflowers and fall tree colors are attractions on this all-day trip.

23. JAKES CREEK FALLS

3.2 miles roundtrip

Allow 3 hours

Elementary schoolers and older children will enjoy this hike from a historic community to a historic cabin and a waterfall.

How to Get There: Turn onto the Elkmont Road off the Little River Road. Drive beside the Little River. Just before the campground entrance, turn left. Pass the trailhead for the Elkmont Nature Trail on the left, opposite the campground. Continue past the parking areas for the Little River Trail. Drive through the old Appalachian Club community and park at the parking lot. The nearest restrooms are about 200 yards below the parking area, at the Appalachian Clubhouse parking area. (These are closed in the winter). Other nearby restrooms are in the Elkmont Campground/Picnic Area.

Description of the Hike: Start at the gated trailhead. Ascend an old roadbed amid chimneys and one house. When the old roadbed forks, go to the left. At 0.7 miles, the Cucumber Gap Trail leaves to the left. The Meigs Mountain Trail veers off to the right at 0.8 miles. Stay on the Jakes Creek Trail. The sound of Jakes Creek drifts up through the hemlock and rhododendron from the right and below the trail.

At 0.25 miles past the junction with Meigs Mountain Trail (about 1 mile from the parking area), a small, unmarked trail descends some steps on the right to Jakes Creek. Cross the footlog and climb the side of the ridge to the Avent Cabin.

The one-room cabin was built from poplar logs by the Ownby family around 1850. Originally, there were one window and one door in the cabin with no stone fireplace. Frank and Mayna Avent bought the cabin for $200 from the Ownby family in 1918. Mayna Avent, a well-known artist, began using the cabin as a studio in 1919. The Avent Cabin is the only original dwelling in the Jakes Creek/Elkmont area. The Avents altered the cabin by adding a large window on one end of the house and a small kitchen on the other end. This is a beautiful spot that inspired some of Mayna Avent's art. Return to Jakes Creek Trail by the same narrow side trail. At the main trail, continue to the right.

In places, fine-grained Thunderhead Sandstone crowds the trail on the left. At 1.6 miles, just before a footlog crosses Waterdog Branch, a small side trail drops off the roadbed to Jakes Creek Falls, a 6-foot waterfall. The large plunge pool below the falls is a good place to splash around on a hot summer day. Return to the car by the same route.

24. LITTLE RIVER AND CUCUMBER GAP

6 miles roundtrip

Allow 4 to 5 hours

Elementary schoolers and older children will enjoy this walk beside the Little River and through the remnants of cabins and old houses of Elkmont.

How to Get There: Go 5 miles on the Little River Road from Sugarlands Visitor Center toward Townsend and Cades Cove. Turn into the Elkmont area and follow the Little River toward the campground. Just before the campground entrance, turn left. You will pass around the campground and by the trailhead for the Elkmont Nature Trail on the left. Park at the first parking area on the left, opposite the intersection beyond the campground. The road continues past the intersection to the Jakes Creek Trailhead, but this walk begins at the Little River Trailhead beyond the barrier near the first parking area. The nearest restrooms are beside the old Appalachian Clubhouse just 0.1 miles beyond this parking area, near the upper parking area. (These are closed in the winter). There are also restrooms in Elkmont Campground.

Description of the Hike: Walk beside the Little River through the upper part of the Elkmont community on what was once a railroad bed used by the logging industry in the early years of the twentieth century. The Elkmont area is interesting with many houses and cabins still intact and many that are simply a chimney or other remnants.

About 150 yards from the trailhead, a gravel roadway goes off to the right. Wander down this little "detour" to what is fondly called the Troll Bridge, a small stone walking bridge that leads to an old house site. This is a fun spot for children. Walk back out to the main trail to continue.

At just a little over 2 miles, the trail crosses Huskey Branch. A nice cascade tumbles down from the right of the trail to spill into the Little River. Continue past the cascade to the junction of Cucumber Gap Trail at 2.4 miles. Turn right onto the Cucumber Gap Trail and ascend into a second-growth forest with rhododendron and hemlock.

At 2.6 miles (0.3 miles from the trail junction), rock hop the same Huskey Branch that you saw below. Look at the doghobble and ferns that crowd the trail as you ascend to Cucumber Gap at 3.7 miles. When the leaves are off the trees you can see Burnt Mountain and Bear Wallow Creek.

This area was logged many years ago, but some large tulip trees are still around. Walk down from Cucumber Gap and cross Tulip Branch (once called Poplar Branch) before the trail's junction with the Jakes Creek Trail. Jakes Creek Falls is 0.9 miles to the left; but to complete the loop, turn right and descend on the gravel roadbed to the old Elkmont Road. Walk down the road through the chimneys and cabin remnants of a bygone era. The David Chapman cabin still stands. (*Do not* go in; but enjoy it from the trail.) Colonel David Chapman was one of the leading advocates to establish Great Smoky Mountains National Park.

When you come to the gate and the upper parking area, walk down the right fork of the paved road 0.1 miles back to your car at the Little River Trailhead (although either fork will deliver you back to your car).

25. HUSKEY BRANCH FALLS

4.3 miles roundtrip

Allow 2.5 to 3 hours

Preschoolers and older children can enjoy this easy hike beside the Little River to a small cascade.

How to Get There: Go 5 miles on the Little River Road from Sugarlands Visitor Center toward Townsend and Cades Cove. Turn into the Elkmont area and pass the campground by turning left. Pass the trailhead for the Elkmont Nature Trail on the left and park at the first parking area beyond the campground. The road continues past the intersection to Jakes Creek, but this walk begins at the Little River Trailhead on the roadbed beyond the barrier, past the parking area.

Description of the Hike: The Little River Trail was once a railroad bed used by the logging industry in the early years of the twentieth century. After about 150 yards, a gravel roadbed goes off to the right. A small stone bridge, some call the Troll Bridge, is a nice stop for children. The bridge is only about 50 yards off the main trail near an old house site.

The main trail parallels the Little River and is an easy walk because it climbs only 300 feet in just a little over 2 miles. Benches along the way provide nice opportunities to enjoy the river. Icicles cling to the rocky cliffs on the right side of the trail in the cold winter months. Wildflowers abound in the spring and summer. Fall's show of color is particularly pretty in this hardwood forest.

Huskey Branch is a pleasant stream that slides down bare metasandstone into the Little River. Rhododendrons crowd around this small cascade. Although not as spectacular as others, this quiet spot is easy to reach, and even smaller children will enjoy it. Look for trout in the stream along the way.

The Huskey name comes from families that lived in the area. Sam Huskey had a store in Sugarlands. Enjoy this walk in any season. It is a nice complement to the Elkmont Nature Trail, the Jakes Creek Falls, the longer Little River/Cucumber Gap Trail, or the drive between Gatlinburg and Townsend.

26. CURRY MOUNTAIN

7 miles roundtrip

Allow 4 to 5 hours

Older children and **teens** will be challenged by this walk up an old roadbed to a cemetery.

How to Get There: Park at the Metcalf Bottoms Picnic Area because there is no parking available at the trailhead. Walk east (left) out of the picnic area 0.2 miles to the trailhead beside the Little River Road (be careful of traffic). The trailhead is located on the south side of the road. Metcalf Bottoms Picnic Area is 8 miles from the Townsend Y and 9.3 miles from Sugarlands Visitor Center.

Description of the Hike: The 1,100-foot elevation gain on this trail is gradual with the steepest part coming in the first 0.5 miles (the trail ascends more than 500 feet during the first 0.8 miles). Some sections are relatively level as the trail follows an old logging road. The first mile of this hike parallels the Little River and Little River Road; glimpses of both are visible from the trail. The roar of the river below drowns out most of the traffic noise. Without summer foliage blocking the views, you will have sporadic glimpses of Wears Valley and some of the surrounding mountains as you ascend this first section of trail.

This trail passes through several rhododendron tunnels as well as hardwood and hemlock forests. You will cross a few small, wet areas that vary in size depending on the recent rainfall. Notice that many of the hemlocks are dead or dying from the hemlock woolly adelgid.

At 2.5 miles, you will cross Curry Gap and make a sharp turn to the right. The next 0.5-mile stretch offers great views of the surrounding mountains to the east, including Bullhead and Mt. LeConte in the distance. The name Curry comes from a Cherokee word *Guri* for a plant used for spring salads. The story is that a Cherokee identified this area as *Guri-hi* ("the *Guri* is there"). The mountain became known as Curry He. The adjoining peak on the other side of Curry Gap was called Curry She for fun.

At 3.3 miles, you arrive at the junction with Meigs Mountain Trail. Turn right onto Meigs Mountain Trail for a few hundred yards to see the Meigs Mountain Cemetery. Return to your car by the same route.

If you have two cars in your group, you have several options for creating a longer one-way hike. One option is to continue on 6 more miles toward the Great Smoky Mountains Institute at Tremont via the Meigs Mountain and Lumber Ridge Trails. You could also take the Meigs Creek Trail 5.4 more miles to the Sinks. Or you could hike eastbound 5 more miles along the Meigs Mountain Trail to Elkmont.

27. LITTLE GREENBRIER SCHOOL
AND WALKER SISTERS' HOUSE

4 miles roundtrip

Allow 3 to 3.5 hours

Preschoolers and older children will like this easy hike to an old school and log house. The trail gains only about 360 feet in 2 miles. This hike offers historical structures and streams.

How to Get There: The trailhead is at the Metcalf Bottoms Picnic Area on the Little River Road, 9.3 miles from the Sugarlands Visitor Center near Gatlinburg and 8 miles from the Townsend Y. Restrooms are available at the picnic area, and there is a pit toilet at the schoolhouse.

Description of the Hike: Park at the Metcalf Bottoms Picnic Area, which is named for the family that once farmed this flat, open area. Enjoy a picnic or a splash in the river before crossing the bridge over the Little River. The trail starts across the river at a gated, gravel jeep road on the right. After 50 yards, the gravel road turns to the left. Gradually ascend the gravel roadbed. Notice the stones of an old home place on the left. Spanish bayonet and daffodils decorate the old house site. Continue on the gravel road through mountain laurel and hemlock to an old cistern that once provided the water for Metcalf Bottoms.

Bear to the right onto a footpath through pine, hardwoods, and rhododendron. Descend to a flat area of mostly second-growth forest that was once farmed. The trail follows Little Brier Creek, where spring wildflowers abound. Cross a footlog at 0.9 miles; then recross the creek on another footlog in sight of Little Greenbrier Schoolhouse.

Little Greenbrier School.

This old log building, built in 1882, was used as a school and Primitive Baptist Church until 1935, when the area became part of the park. Imagining what school life was like in those days is made easier by the period furniture and interpretive programs. Buried in the cemetery at the church/school are many Walkers and Kings who lived in the Little Greenbrier area. The number of children's graves indicates how hard mountain life must have been.

Continue through the parking lot and up the gravel road. Leave the main road onto another gravel road that turns to the right above the schoolhouse and cemetery. Go past the gate 0.75 miles to a split in the road. The roadbed without gravel continues 0.25 miles up to Little Brier Gap with nice views of Wears Cove. However, to reach the log house of the Walker sisters, turn right on the gravel road at the split. The Walker Sisters' House is 2 miles from the Metcalf Bottoms Picnic Area and 1.1 miles from Little Greenbrier Schoolhouse.

The log house and surrounding buildings were built soon after the Civil War by John and Margaret Walker who had 11 children. Five of their children, all girls, never married and lived in the house. The Walker sisters, Hettie, Margaret Jane, Polly, Louisa Susan, and Martha Ann did not deed the house over to the national park until 1941, with the condition that they be permitted to live there until their deaths. The last sister, Louisa Susan, died in 1964 at the age of 82.

Walker Sisters Cabin, October 11, 1952. Albert "Dutch" Roth Photograph Collection, University of Tennessee, Knoxville Libraries.

The sisters welcomed hikers and tourists, allowing them to observe their self-sufficient life style. Let your children roam through the house and over the small farm. Look at the springhouse that doubled as refrigerator and water faucet. A corn crib/shed stored the harvest from the cleared land. The spring has a special charm when the sisters' daffodils are in bloom. Return to Metcalf Bottoms by the same route.

It is possible to park at the schoolhouse and walk only the 1.1-mile section to the Walker Sisters' House. A gravel road from the Metcalf Bottoms–Wears Valley Road leads up to the schoolhouse. This gravel road is narrow, and it is difficult to pass oncoming cars. It may be necessary to back up to allow a car to pass.

This area is popular and can be crowded. Many picnic and play in the Little River at the Metcalf Bottoms Picnic Area.

28. UPPER MEIGS FALLS

3.6 miles roundtrip

Allow 2 to 3 hours

Although this a moderate trail, it is recommended for older **elementary schoolers** and older children because the four rock hops across Meigs Creek can be difficult, especially with high water flow. It offers wildflowers, a pleasant creek, a waterfall, and a chance to watch kayakers.

How to Get There: The hike to Upper Meigs Falls is on the Meigs Creek Trail. Park at the Sinks on Little River Road (TN 73), 12 miles west of the Sugarlands Visitor Center and 6 miles east of the Y in Townsend.

Description of the Hike: This is a nice walk in all seasons. Stopping at the Sinks can be a treat in itself, a beautiful spot to watch the Little River drop about 12 feet over a ledge of large boulders into a deep pool. The area around the parking lot contains several boulders that make good places for a picnic and a chance to watch kayakers come through the rapids, especially when the water flow is high. The parking area can be crowded, especially on weekends.

The Meigs Creek Trail starts with a short climb above the Sinks, then descends to a low, swampy area about 0.1 miles from the parking lot. After a right turn, the trail ascends a ridge that roughly parallels the Little River and Little River Road. You can hear the sounds of traffic and water

Creek play at one of the park's many waterfalls entertains young and old alike.

as you climb the ridge through a cove hardwood forest. In springtime this area has a wide variety of wildflowers. You will reach the ridge crest at about 0.9 miles, where a left turn, around the ridge, takes you away from Little River. The forest is now much different than that on the other side of the ridge. The dry southwest exposure here supports pine, oak, and maple trees, as well as the understory of mountain laurel, huckle- berry, and galax.

Descending the ridge for about 0.5 miles, the trail enters tulip tree, hemlock, and rhododendron along Meigs Creek. At 1.4 miles, you reach the first of four creek crossings. Be cautious—the crossings can be chal- lenging. The trail now follows Meigs Creek through rhododendron and crosses the creek three more times in short succession. After the fourth crossing, at about 1.75 miles, the trail climbs slightly for 200 yards before reaching the side trail to the falls on the right. Although Upper Meigs Falls can be seen from the trail, the best views and photo opportunities are from the base down the short, but steep side trail. The rocks around the falls are usually wet from spray or high water, making this a poor place for a break.

Meigs Creek and Falls are named for Return Jonathan Meigs, a Revolutionary War officer, who served as Cherokee Indian Agent from 1801 until his death in 1823. While agent to the Cherokee, he worked to help them assimilate with white settlers and to establish their own form of government that was loosely based on the new US Constitution. An early boundary line between Tennessee and the Cherokee nation, called the Meigs Line, passed near this trail that now bears his name.

Return to the parking area by the same route. There are several places along the creek or on the ridge for a nice break.

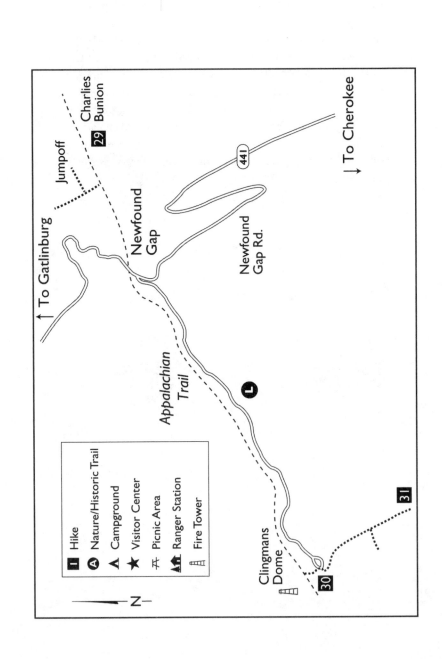

Newfound Gap–
Clingmans Dome

US Highway 441 passes over the crest of the Smokies at Newfound Gap about halfway between Cherokee, North Carolina, and Gatlinburg, Tennessee. The original road over the Smokies passed just a few miles west of Newfound Gap at Indian Gap. Remnants of this old route still exist along the Road Prong Trail. The "new" highway was built in the 1930s through the newly established Great Smoky Mountains National Park. The over 2,100-mile Appalachian Trail (A.T.) crosses US 441 at Newfound Gap (5,046 feet above sea level). The gap straddles the Tennessee–North Carolina state line.

It was at the Rockefeller Memorial at Newfound Gap that President Franklin D. Roosevelt dedicated the park on September 2, 1940, with his right foot in Tennessee and his left foot in North Carolina. The memorial plaque at Newfound Gap commemorates a gift from the Laura Spellman Rockefeller Memorial Fund that helped to acquire land for the park. Children enjoy climbing the steps to the spot where the president stood.

At 6,643 feet, Clingmans Dome is the highest peak in the Great Smoky Mountains National Park. Despite its great height, it is the most accessible summit because you can drive nearly to the top. An observation tower at the top affords fantastic views that are available to everyone. Turn onto the 7-mile Clingmans Dome Road as it leaves US 441 near Newfound Gap. This intersection is 19 miles from Cherokee and 22 miles from Gatlinburg. The Clingmans Dome Road is closed in the winter (from December 1 to April 1). Parking is available at the Forney Ridge Parking Area, which has four pit toilet restrooms. At peak times (holidays and weekends in fall leaf season), parking areas can be crowded. A small visitor center and gift shop are located at the beginning of the Clingmans Dome Trail.

In addition to being the highest point in the park, Clingmans Dome is also the highest point in Tennessee and on the A.T. The A.T. is a national public scenic footpath that begins at Springer Mountain in Georgia and traverses the Appalachians over 2,190 miles to Mt. Katahdin

Franklin D. Roosevelt, Newfound Gap. Thompson
Brothers Photograph Collection, University of Tennessee,
Knoxville Libraries.

in Maine. Seventy-two miles of the Appalachian Trail is within Great
Smoky Mountains National Park.

The Cherokee called this peak *Kuwahi*, or Mulberry Place. The Cherokee believed bears met on this mountain for dances just before entering their winter's den. Also, it was thought that bears came to a nearby
enchanted lake known as *Attahahi* to be healed of wounds. Hunters
could not see this invisible lake.

Later, Euro-American settlers called this peak Smoky Dome due
to the fog and clouds that hung like smoke on the rounded dome. This
name officially changed in 1859 when Arnold Guyot, an early explorer
and mapmaker, wrote Thomas Lanier Clingman's (1812-1897) name on
his map of the Smokies. Clingman had explored the Black Mountains
and the Smokies in the 1840s and 1850s.

In 1937, the Civilian Conservation Corps built the first tower open
to the public on Clingmans Dome; it was constructed of wood. The current concrete spiral tower at the peak was completed in 1960 around the

same time the Clingmans Dome Road was paved. The concrete tower benefited from some needed improvements and renovations in 2018.

Flowers are beautiful throughout the growing season. Balsam snake root, yarrow, crimson bee balm, golden ragwort, mountain ash, and more are visible along the trails. The tiny spruce-fir moss spider (about one-eighth inch long), an endangered species, is actually a tarantula! It is extremely rare and only found on a few peaks in the Southern Appalachians. In the fall, blackberries (briarless), blueberries, and mountain ash berries ripen and attract bears who are gorging for the long winter.

The dead trees visible are mostly Fraser fir that have been attacked since the 1950s by a tiny insect, the balsam woolly adelgid. New trees continue to grow, but the bug is still present. The red spruce, also a part of this forest, has a symbiotic relationship with the Fraser fir and is under stress as well.

At Clingmans Dome, spring arrives late (late May–early June) and winter comes early (late October–early November). Temperatures can be 20 degrees cooler than in the valley. Be prepared for all types of weather by dressing in layers. The peak can often be shrouded in clouds and fog even when it is clear in the valley below. If your stay in the park is limited, Clingmans Dome and Newfound Gap are must-see destinations.

29. CHARLIES BUNION AND THE JUMPOFF

10 miles roundtrip

Allow 6 to 7 hours

Older elementary schoolers and **teens** will find this moderate hike a challenge. About 1,120 feet of elevation is gained over 3 miles, but 600 feet is lost down to Charlies Bunion. This hike offers magnificent views!

How to Get There: The trailhead is at Newfound Gap off US 441, 15 miles from Gatlinburg and 18 miles from Cherokee. Good restrooms are available at Newfound Gap.

Description of the Hike: Take the Appalachian Trail (A.T.) east from the parking lot at Newfound Gap. This walk is part of the over 2,100-mile A.T., which stretches along the crest of the Appalachians from Georgia to Maine and is marked with white blazes on trees and rocks. The walk to Charlies Bunion is most difficult at the beginning.

The first 2.5 miles is mostly uphill through some old-growth forest. The trail is rocky with many roots, so walk carefully and do not rush. Red spruce and Fraser fir are abundant as the trail straddles the North Carolina–Tennessee state line. Children will enjoy standing in both states at the same time. North Carolina is to the south and east while Tennessee lies to the north and west.

At 0.5 miles is a good view of the Tennessee Smokies, Mt. LeConte, and the Chimneys. Continue the ascent of Mt. Kephart, named for the famed outdoors writer Horace Kephart, who actively supported the establishment of a national park in the Smokies. Kephart did not live to see President Franklin D. Roosevelt dedicate the park at Newfound Gap in 1940.

At 1.7 miles, the Sweat Heifer Trail leaves the A.T. and goes 3.7 miles to the right to the Kephart Prong Shelter. Follow the A.T. here as it moderates considerably along the top of a ridge to the summit of Mt. Kephart

A hike in the Smokies is fun in any season.

(6,150 feet above sea level). As blackberry briars crowd the trail along this stretch, look for the dark-eyed junco, a small, gray bird that flits about mountain summits. Mountain folk called the junco "snowbirds" because they migrate to the valleys when there is snow on the top of the mountains. We sometimes run across grouse and red squirrel on this particular walk. A grouse will flap its wings against the ground as it takes off, making a *boom* to scare and distract any intruder.

The summit of Mt. Kephart provides good views of North Carolina. The Boulevard Trail to Mt. LeConte (5.2 miles away) breaks off to the left at 2.6 miles. (The Jumpoff offers a spectacular view 0.5 miles from this trail junction. See below). Take the right fork and descend to the Ice Water Springs Shelter, a three-sided stone shelter that can sleep 12. Reservations through the Backcountry Information Office are required for this often-crowded shelter. Do not drink the water from Ice Water Spring unless you treat it properly. It looks inviting but could cause illness. The last mile to Charlies Bunion is mostly downhill along a rocky trail.

Charlies Bunion is a rocky outcrop that was denuded by a forest fire in 1925. Heavy rains and winds scoured the summit, which Horace Kephart supposedly named for Charlie Conner. The story is that in 1929, as they rested on the rocky outcrop, Charlie Conner removed his boot and revealed a bruised bunion.

The views are spectacular! To the northeast is the Jumpoff and Mt. LeConte with Horseshoe Mountain and Greenbrier Pinnacle to the north. Mt. Guyot, Old Black, and Mt. Chapman are to the northeast. To the south is Richland Mountain, Thomas Divide, and the Qualla Boundary. *Caution: do not climb too near the edge!!*

Return to Newfound Gap by the same route. The best time of the year for this hike is between late spring and early fall. The trail can be icy and dangerous during the winter. It is cool amid the mountain breezes in the summer. Sometimes it snows as late as early May. Do not miss Charlies Bunion, one of the best views in the Smokies.

THE JUMPOFF

The Boulevard Trail, which goes 5.2 miles to Mt. LeConte, leaves the A.T. at 2.7 miles from Newfound Gap. Walk on the Boulevard Trail about 100 paces, looking carefully for the sign to the Jumpoff. The trail, which angles off to the right, is narrow and slightly rough. The Jumpoff is less than 0.5 miles from the sign. Blackberry bushes at the beginning give way to a spruce-fir forest.

The cliffs provide an excellent view to the north and east. Charlies Bunion along the A.T. and Porters Creek can be seen below. Greenbrier Pinnacle, Old Black, Mt. Guyot, and Mt. Chapman are also sights from this cliff top. Once, we started on a pretty fall day only to ascend into clouds. When we arrived at the Jumpoff, it was so foggy that nothing could be seen. An eight-year-old gasped, "It's the edge of the world!" There was no horizon, no valley, no sky—only gray fog.

Summer has the most haze from poor air quality and the most possibilities for afternoon thunderstorms. Remember that it is cool on the top of the Smokies. A trip in late May can mean early spring weather. The Jumpoff is an easy side trip that is well worth the time on the way to or from Charlies Bunion or Mt. LeConte, or it can be a great trip in its own right.

30. CLINGMANS DOME

1 mile roundtrip

Allow 45 minutes to 1 hour

Preschoolers and **elementary schoolers** will enjoy the views from the tower on this moderate hike that gains 330 feet in 0.5 miles. Frequent stops are a great idea. Often it is the parent that struggles in the higher altitude. A sign at the base of the paved trail does not recommend strollers. The hike offers fine views and a close-up look at the spruce-fir forest.

How to Get There: The trail begins at the Forney Ridge Parking Area at the end of the Clingmans Dome Road, 7 miles from Newfound Gap Road.

Description of the Hike: The trail is paved all the way to the top. The spruce-fir forest through which the trail ascends is dying due to an infestation of balsam woolly adelgids and to acid rain. Over 95% of the mature Fraser fir trees have been affected by the tiny insect. Studies of the effects of acid rain and air quality are being conducted near the summit of Clingmans Dome. Park resource managers are trying to save some of the surviving trees. The Fraser fir grows only in the Southern Appalachians and is a candidate for listing as an endangered species.

Benches and interpretive signs offer opportunities to rest on the way up. Do not rush in the thinner air of the high Smokies. You are over 1,000 feet higher than Denver, Colorado! Enjoy the smell of the spruce-fir forest and the sound of birdsong.

The tower at the summit affords great 360-degree views. Picture maps orient the observer to the surrounding peaks, which are magnificent on clear days. Remember, however, that just because it's clear in the valley doesn't mean it's clear at the summit, which can often be cloaked in fog. The return to the car is easy.

In the winter, the summit can only be reached by a 7-mile, one-way walk since the road is closed due to ice and snow. The Appalachian Trail reaches the highest point of its entire length (over 2,100 miles) when it crosses the summit only a few yards from the base of the observation tower.

One experiment we enjoy is sealing an empty water bottle in Gatlinburg or Cherokee and listening to it pop when it's opened at the summit. This is due to the great change in air pressure. Another way to illustrate this is to partially fill a balloon in the lowlands and watch it fill out as the car climbs.

The drive over Newfound Gap along US 441 and on the Clingmans Dome Road offers the only place in the park to ride through the northern spruce-fir forest. It is said that driving from Gatlinburg or Cherokee to Newfound Gap exposes one to the same climate change as driving from Tennessee or North Carolina to southern Canada. While at Clingmans Dome, walk to Andrews Bald and the Spruce-Fir Nature Trail.

31. ANDREWS BALD

4.2 miles roundtrip

Allow 3 to 4 hours

Elementary schoolers will enjoy this moderate hike that descends 630 feet to a grassy bald, excellent views, and spring flowers.

How to Get There: The hike begins at the Forney Ridge Parking Area at the end of the Clingmans Dome Road.

Description of the Hike: Use the Forney Ridge Trail that begins to the left of the paved trail to Clingmans Dome. The Forney Ridge Trail is a rocky footpath that can be difficult for little feet to negotiate and is therefore not recommended for preschool children. At 0.1 miles, the trail divides. Take a left at the sign (straight ahead leads to the Appalachian Trail).

For 0.9 miles, the trail descends along the western slope of Forney Ridge, which burned in the 1920s. Some Fraser firs are still living in spite of the balsam woolly adelgid, but many of the trees are dead or dying. The red spruce still populate the forest.

At 1 mile, the trail surface becomes easier to walk. As the trail continues along the crest of Forney Ridge, the forest becomes denser. At 1.1 miles, the Forney Creek Trail goes to the right on its way to Fontana Lake 11 miles away. The last mile in the spruce-fir forest is very pleasant with many ferns. From the bald, enjoy the great views of Fontana Lake and the North Carolina mountains to the south and east. The Smokies' crest is easily seen to the west.

This large grassy bald has a wonderful show of flame azalea and rhododendron in June. The faint, sweet smell of rhododendron and blackberry blossoms hangs in the fresh mountain air. Andres Thompson, a Confederate volunteer who settled in the valley below in the 1850s, grazed his cattle on the bald. The bald was called "Andres' Bald," but a mapmaker wrote it down as Andrews and the name stuck.

The blueberries that ripen in September provide a tasty snack. Children love this spot because they have the feeling they are on top of the world. They romp, play, and run in the thick grass. Take lunch and allow plenty of time. Ponder the expanse of the mountains and nature itself as your children explore. From spring to late fall, one can hardly go wrong with this hike. Andrews Bald, in combination with Clingmans Dome Tower and the Spruce-Fir Nature Trail, makes a wonderful day of experiencing the beauty and grandeur of the Great Smoky Mountains. This is the easiest bald for children to reach. If you have only one day and can take only one hike, Andrews Bald may be your best choice.

Watch the weather which can change quickly. Always carry rain gear, particularly in the summer when afternoon thunderstorms can pop up. This trail benefited from a reconstruction through the Friends of the Smokies' Trails Forever program.

Cades Cove–Townsend

Cades Cove is a picturesque mountain valley in the western part of the park. Its popularity is due to outstanding scenery and plentiful wildlife. The 11-mile loop road is a popular auto trail, especially in the fall. The Cades Cove Visitor Center is located midway on the one-way loop road at Cable Mill. Townsend, once a logging center, is a small town at the entrance of the Great Smoky Mountains National Park nearest Cades Cove.

US Highway 321 runs 20 miles from Maryville and 15 miles from Pigeon Forge to Townsend. From Gatlinburg, take Little River Road 18 miles to the Y, which is an intersection of roads and streams that is very popular for picnicking, swimming, and tubing. From there, it is only 7 more miles to Cades Cove, where there is a campground and picnic area with restrooms.

Laurel Creek Road is the only way into the cove, but there is an additional way out that is a one-way gravel road. Rich Mountain Road begins at the Missionary Baptist Church and goes over Rich Mountain to Townsend. Rich Mountain is closed to vehicle travel in the winter. Another route, Parson's Branch, once traversed Hannah Mountain to US 129 at Chilhowee Lake. It has been closed for years. It can be walked or biked but is not open to vehicles at the time of this writing.

The Cherokee had a settlement in the cove called "Otter Place." This settlement was occupied even after people of European descent began to farm the area. Some say that the cove was named after Cherokee Chief Kade while others maintain that it was named for Chief Abraham's wife, Kate. In either case, the name was derived from the original inhabitants, the Cherokee.

Because of its popularity, Cades Cove can be very crowded. Plan to arrive early in the morning to avoid traffic and to see the most wildlife. Deer, bear, fox, turkeys, groundhogs, and more can be seen from your car. Bicycling allows you to experience the cove at a slower pace. Bicycles can be rented from the store near the Cades Cove Campground. The loop road is closed on Wednesdays to all motor vehicles. This is a wonderful opportunity to bike or walk the loop. Two gravel roads, Hyatt and Sparks Lanes, cut across from the north to the south side of the cove,

To Maryville

Foothills Parkway

Hike
Nature/Historic Trail
Campground
Visitor Center
Picnic Area
Ranger Station
Fire Tower

Look Rock

Foothills
Pkwy.

N

321

42

Townsend

321

To Pigeon
Forge

Abrams Creek

Closed in
winter

Rich Mtn.
Rd.

Little
River Rd. To
Gatlinburg

One
Way

37

32

35

Great Smoky
Mtn. Institute

39

36

40

33

Cades Cove

Tremont

129

Parsons Branch

Forge Creek
Rd.

38

34

To Fontana

41

*Parsons Branch currently closed

allowing the trip to be shortened. Horseback riding is also available. From March to October, hayrides are available in Cades Cove at the riding stables (865-448-9009). All seasons are beautiful in the cove.

Numerous cabins and other buildings show how life was lived in Cades Cove in the 1800s. At the time the park was established, hundreds of people lived there. Schools, churches, and stores were all present as were framed houses. Most of these were removed after the establishment of the park. A Civilian Conservation Corps camp was in the cove just beyond the Missionary Baptist Church. The last residents to live in Cades Cove left in 2001 following the death of the lease holder. Today, visitors can look back in time to a moment in the area's history.

Townsend has been home to humans for thousands of years. Visit the Great Smoky Mountain Heritage Center to see exhibits of the area's history from earliest times to the present. Bus tours of Cades Cove are offered through the Great Smoky Mountain Heritage Center. The west end of the park offers many great hiking, biking, and touring opportunities.

32. CHESTNUT TOP

1 mile roundtrip

Allow 1.5 to 2 hours

Elementary schoolers will like the challenge of this moderate hike through an amazing display of wildflowers.

How to Get There: Enter the park through the Townsend entrance. The parking area is on the left (by the Little River) between the park entrance and the Townsend Y. The trailhead is across the road from the parking area. This parking area can be crowded with people tubing and swimming at the Y.

Description of Hike: In the spring, this short walk has one of the most amazing displays of wildflowers in the entire park. Once we counted nearly 30 wildflower species in one walk! This hike goes up the side of Chestnut Top Ridge. Take it slow. Do not rush. The wonder of this walk is the wildflowers. The show begins in mid-March and runs through April. Different weeks mean different flowers. The early flowers, such as trailing arbutus and hepatica, come in March with many others to follow.

Help your children to see that as you walk uphill, you walk back in time. The flowers that are blooming at the top already bloomed down near the road a week or two before. Also, notice the leaves on the trees as you ascend.

Begin the walk across the busy road from the parking area. Simply walk the trail 0.5 miles to the top of the ridge, then turn around and come back to your car. With more adventurous children, you can continue to walk on the Chestnut Top Trail for however long you want to go. The top of the ridge is in a pine-oak forest with mountain laurel.

This short hike is one that we sometimes take several times each spring simply to see the wildflower show.

33. SPRUCE FLATS FALLS

2 miles roundtrip

Allow 1.5 to 2 hours

Elementary schoolers will like the challenge of this moderate hike to a gorgeous set of waterfalls.

Black bear.

Bear Facts

The black bear is *the* symbol of the Great Smoky Mountains. Once black bears lived in most of North America. Now their wild range in the eastern United States is limited to only a few places. The population varies from year to year. In recent years, about 1,600 bears lived in Great Smoky Mountains National Park.

Adult males can weigh about 250 pounds in the summer but can double their weight by fall as they gorge for the long winter. Bears weigh about 8 ounces at birth and some have been known to weigh more than 600 pounds as adults!

A bear can live from 12 to 15 years. Like humans, they are omnivorous—meaning they eat just about anything. A bear can run about 30 miles per hour, which is faster than a human.

How to Get There: From the intersection of Little River Road and Laurel Creek Road, go 0.2 miles west toward Cades Cove and turn at the Tremont sign. Follow the Tremont Road 2 miles to the Great Smoky Mountains Institute. Turn left, cross the bridge, and park in the Institute parking lot. The resource center is a gift shop with books, posters, and resources on the park, as well as restrooms.

Description of Hike: Walk on the road from the parking area. The trail is to the left, before the Tremont Institute buildings. Signs direct you up and around the Institute. Do not get discouraged with the steepness at the beginning. Several signs mark the way. The trail is high (sometimes more than 300 feet) above the Middle Prong of the Little River. You will cross a few wet-weather branches that drain the steep slopes of Mill Ridge.

Do not allow children to get too far ahead or behind. The ridge side is steep. Continue along the trail through mountain laurel and pine to where Spruce Flats Branch joins the Middle Prong of the Little River. The trail arrives at the fourth in a series of falls that drops nearly 125 feet in a short distance. The base of the falls here is 60 feet wide with a large plunge pool that temporarily holds the water as it pushes on to the Little River. Some of the upper falls can be seen from a vantage point at the lowest falls. *Do not attempt to climb to the other falls.* Thunderhead Sandstone, which is very resistant to erosion and is streaked with quartz, makes up the cliffs near the falls.

Notice the rocks on the left side of the falls are more rounded than the jumble of rocks on the slope to the right. The more angular stones were chipped and blasted from the cliffs above to build a logging railroad bed, which is about 100 feet above the lowest falls on the side opposite the trail. The smoother stones were worn down by the water.

This area was one of the last logged by the Little River Logging Company. Early efforts to cut timber near here were thwarted by Will Walker who, in 1859, settled the flat area where the Great Smoky Mountain Institute now stands. Walker did not sell the timber rights to the area until just before his death in 1920.

The Great Smoky Mountains Institute at Tremont is an environmental education center. It offers educational opportunities year-round for all ages. Inquire at the office or check online at www.gsmit.org. Children have long played and learned in this area since Will Walker raised his family in Walker Valley. Camp Margaret Townsend, a Girl Scout camp in the 1920s and 1930s, stood on the same site. The Institute now serves children who come with school groups to learn more about the environment and the Great Smoky Mountains.

Return by the same route to your car. The trail is well traveled but rarely crowded. This is an undiscovered jewel in the park. It is a good complement to the Lynn Camp Prong Cascade hike and the Tremont Logging Auto Tour.

34. LYNN CAMP PRONG

1.5 miles roundtrip

Allow 1.5 to 2 hours

Preschoolers and **elementary schoolers** will enjoy this walk that is slightly uphill. This hike offers waterfalls, creeks, colorful fall leaves, and spring wildflowers.

How to Get There: From the intersection of Little River Road and Laurel Creek Road, drive 0.2 miles west toward Cades Cove and turn at the Tremont sign. Follow the Tremont Road 2 miles to the entrance to the Great Smoky Mountains Institute. On the right side of the road, you can purchase a booklet about logging in the Tremont area for a small fee. Follow the gravel road 3 miles until it ends at a turnaround. Park here. The nearest restrooms are in the resource center at the Great Smoky Mountains Institute.

Description of the Hike: Cross the footbridge over Lynn Camp Prong to an old railroad bed that splits in two directions. At the trail intersection, take the left fork, which follows the creek along the Middle Prong Trail. The trail is a gravel roadbed that is open to horses (watch your step). It is possible to take a stroller along this section. Ferns, doghobble, fire cherry, and rhododendron are mixed with the hardwood forest.

After 0.3 miles, a bench on the left has a good view of a large cascade. Proceed to a second bench that overlooks the middle of the cascade. An overhanging rock provides a vantage point of the water as it rushes past. Hang on to small hands! We often throw sticks in and watch them float on the swift water. Look for trout in the mountain stream.

Sixty paces beyond the second bench is an 8-foot waterfall. Look for old steel cables leftover from logging days. Below the falls is a wonderful place to cool hot feet or have a picnic.

Another set of cascades is 0.25 miles up the Middle Prong Trail. Two groups of falls form these beautiful cascades. The rocks are moss-covered with rhododendron, beech, and doghobble on the banks. A bench is located near the upper group of falls, 100 feet upstream from the lower set.

Beauty and wonder combine at waterfalls throughout the Smokies.

The Middle Prong Trail continues to the Appalachian Trail 7.5 miles away. Older children may want to walk farther along the creek, while younger ones may be ready to return to the car. The trail is shaded with many good spots for creek play and summer picnics. The hardwood leaves are a good show in the fall, while wildflowers are abundant in the spring. Any season is a good choice for this walk. However, the road to Tremont can be closed in the winter.

The name Lynn Camp perhaps comes from the many linwood (basswood) trees in the area. Or it may come from the Scotch-Irish who settled the mountains. A *lin* (or *linn*) is a small pool in a creek at the base or top of a waterfall. This creek has many a beautiful lin. Enjoy this walk with the *Tremont Logging History* booklet, on the way to Cades Cove, with the Spruce Flats Falls Trail, or just as a day outing on its own.

35. SCHOOLHOUSE GAP, TURKEYPEN RIDGE, FINLEY CANE, AND BOTE MOUNTAIN LOOP

8.8 miles roundtrip

Allow 5 to 6 hours

Teens will like this trek that makes a large loop through the heart of the park's western end. This hike passes old house sites and offers colorful fall leaves and spring wildflowers.

How to Get There: From the intersection of Little River Road and Laurel Creek Road at the Townsend Y, turn onto Laurel Creek Road toward Cades Cove. Travel 3.5 miles west to a parking lot on the right.

Description of the Hike: Begin on the Schoolhouse Gap Trail. The path follows an old roadbed built by Isaac Anderson, the founder of Maryville College. This road, built in the 1830s, was to have gone from the Townsend area through Schoolhouse Gap, up to Spence Field, and down into North Carolina. The story is that Anderson consulted some local Cherokee as to the best route over the mountains. The discussion came down to a choice between two ridges. Anderson asked the Cherokee to vote on which ridge was the better route. There is no *v* sound in the Cherokee language, so the Cherokee took a *bote*. The route that won is still called Bote Mountain Trail (see also Hike #38 on page 81). The Schoolhouse Gap Trail is the northern part of this old trail.

Part of the old road was in Spence Creek (also called Near Creek) that is beside the current trail. Look in the creek for small trenches that are marks of wagon wheels and sleds. Climb to Dosey Gap where the trail levels for a few hundred yards. Dosey Gap is named for local farmer, Anderson Dosey, who fought in the Civil War. At 1.1 miles, turn left onto the Turkeypen Ridge Trail. Climb about 300 feet in elevation over the next 0.75 miles as the trail follows the eastern side of Turkeypen Ridge.

In the spring, flame azalea blazes along the trail. At 2.25 miles from the junction with Schoolhouse Gap Trail, the trail crosses Pinkroot Branch. Pinkroot is a local name for the spring wildflower known as Indian pink. These and other wildflowers abound along this old roadbed that descends into Big Spring Cove. Rock hop over a branch of Laurel Creek in a wet, marshy area where several houses once stood. Notice rock piles that indicate where families cleared fields to farm.

When you are in earshot of the Laurel Creek Road, a trail leaves the main trail to the left. In drier seasons, take the left trail through an old house site (notice artifacts from those who once lived there). In early spring, yellow daffodils indicate where a farm wife once planted them around her doorstep. This side trail goes to a tunnel that drains a branch of Laurel Creek. The water can be high in wet seasons and may make the trail impassable. If it is possible to go through the tunnel, you will emerge onto the Finley Cane Trail.

In wet times, stay on the main Turkeypen Ridge Trail past the Crib Gap Trail, which turns off to the right. The Turkeypen Ridge Trail ends at 3.8 miles at the Laurel Creek Road. Cross the road and take the Finley Cane Trail to the left. Do not get confused here—the Lead Cove Trail goes off to the right.

Finley Cane Trail climbs easily and slowly through rhododendron up the flank of Bote Mountain to intersect Isaac Anderson's old road. You will rock hop across Sugar Cove Prong. At 0.8 miles, you will cross Laurel Cove Creek and Hickory Tree Branch in quick succession. In another mile, you reach Finley Cove Creek which is often dry. A small patch of cane has grown in this area—hence the name—Finley Cane.

Billy Bartram's Travels

In the beginning days of the Revolutionary War, a young botanist from Philadelphia, William Bartram, set out to explore the wilds of the South. His travels brought him south of the Smokies to the Nantahala Gorge where he met the Cherokee chief, Attakullakulla. Bartram was impressed with the wide diversity of plant life in the southern mountains.

Upon seeing flame azalea in bloom, he wrote: "The epithet fiery I annex to this celebrated species of Azalea, as being expressive of the appearance in flower...suddenly opening to the view from dark shades, we are alarmed with the apprehension of the hills being set on fire. This is certainly the most gay and brilliant flowering shrub yet known." Although Bartram never reached what are the present boundaries of the park, he did see the old-growth forest, flame azalea, rhododendron, and other plants and animals that the Great Smoky Mountains National Park now seeks to preserve.

At 2.8 miles from the Laurel Creek Road, you will turn left onto the Bote Mountain Trail—back to Anderson's old 1830s road over the mountain. Follow the roadbed along Bote Mountain. Enjoy views of the high Smokies to the south. West Prong Trail leaves to the right at 0.3 miles from the Finley Cane Trail. It is 1.2 miles down to Laurel Creek Road and your car. The Schoolhouse Gap Trailhead and parking area are just a few hundred yards up the Laurel Creek Road. Use caution crossing the busy, heavily traveled Laurel Creek Road.

This is a wonderful loop trail encompassing 8.8 miles. The circuit covers some beautiful territory in the western end of the park. Take along a picnic lunch.

36. JOHN OLIVER PLACE

0.5 or 3 miles roundtrip
Allow 1 to 3 hours

Preschoolers and **elementary schoolers** will like this easy-to-moderate hike that offers spring wildflowers, fall colors, and a historic cabin.

How to Get There: For the 3-mile hike, park at the beginning of the Cades Cove Loop Road. A sign points to the trailhead past the gate on the right. For the 0.5-mile walk, drive 0.9 miles on the one-way Cades Cove Loop road to a parking area on the right. If this small parking area is full, simply drive on to one of the other pull-offs beyond the parking area. The nearest restrooms are in the picnic area and at the store.

Description of the Hike: Begin the 3-mile hike at the trailhead sign opposite the lower end of the parking area at the start of the Cades Cove Loop Road. This trail is a horse trail as well as a hiking trail. There is no significant elevation gain on this walk. You will walk over three small ridges and cross three small branches. The trail is an old roadbed. Walk to a sign at the junction of Crooked Arm Branch and Rich Mountain Loop Trail.

The crossings of Crooked Arm Branch and Harrison Branch are easy rock hops except in the highest water. Reach the John Oliver Cabin at 1.5 miles. Take time to explore this old homesite of a family who occupied this mountain cove until the 1930s when the park was created. John Oliver was perhaps one of the first to settle Cades Cove, in 1818. The land was not ceded by the Cherokee until 1819, but often settlers of European descent moved onto Indian land. John Oliver's descendants farmed the valley floor for several generations. Let your children tell what they think life was like when this cabin was built in the 1820s. Assist them with questions like: "How did they cook?" "Where did they get their food and clothing?" "Where are the tub and toilet?" Turn around and walk back to the parking area along the same route.

For the 0.5-mile walk, start from the parking area along the Cades Cove Loop Road. Follow the path across the large field up a slight incline to the house. The path is very easy and accessible for all ages. This is a very popular site and can often be crowded. It is where the European settlement of Cades Cove began.

This trail can be abundant in wildlife. We've seen deer, squirrels, chipmunks, and birds, birds, birds. In the fall, the leaf colors and overlooks are exceptional. Spring flowers are abundant, especially near the John Oliver House and Marthas Branch, which is just beyond the house. Spend some time at the John Oliver Place and make a whole day in Cades Cove.

37. RICH MOUNTAIN LOOP

8.7 miles roundtrip

Allow 5 to 6 hours

Older elementary schoolers and **teens** will like this moderate to strenuous hike that gains 1,740 feet in 4 miles. This hike offers spring wildflowers, fall colors, a historic cabin, and scenic views.

How to Get There: Park at the beginning of the Cades Cove Loop Road. A sign points to the trailhead past the gate on the right. The nearest restrooms are in the picnic area and at the store.

Description of the Hike: This trail, which is also a horse trail, is great for a bird's eye view of Cades Cove. Walk the roadbed to a sign at the junction of Crooked Arm Branch and Rich Mountain Loop Trail. This is the beginning and end of the loop trail. To the right is the steepest route, so we suggest going straight and saving the steep part for the downhill leg.

You will reach the John Oliver Cabin at 1.5 miles. Take time to explore this old homesite of a family that occupied this mountain cove until the 1930s when the park was created. John Oliver was perhaps one of the first to settle Cades Cove, in 1818. The land was not ceded by the Cherokee until 1819, but often settlers of European descent moved onto Indian land. John Oliver's descendants farmed the valley floor for several generations. Let your children tell what they think life was like when this cabin was built in the 1820s. Assist them with questions like: "How did they cook?" "Where did they get their food and clothing?" "Where are the tub and toilet?"

At the John Oliver Cabin, the trail turns right to ascend the ridge beside Marthas Branch. The branch was named for one of John and Lucretia Oliver's children. After a few switchbacks, there are good views of Cades Cove.

At 3.4 miles, a sign marks Indian Grave Gap Trail, which runs 1 mile to Rich Mountain Road. Continue 0.8 miles to a trail junction with Rich Mountain Trail. Approximately 0.25 miles beyond this junction is a steep side trail to the left, which goes about 200 yards to the remnants of an old fire tower.

Trees have grown up around this once cleared mountain top. With no leaves in the winter, there are good views of the surrounding mountains. Gregory Bald (southwest) and Thunderhead (southeast) are along the crest of the Smokies. The Chilhowee Mountain range (north) is across Tuckaleechee Cove.

It is 1.8 miles from Rich Mountain Trail to Crooked Arm Ridge Trail. While descending the mountain, notice the great views of Townsend and Walland to the north (left) and Cades Cove to the south (right). You will pass a junction with Scott Mountain Trail on the left. Continue on the Crooked Arm Ridge Trail. Several switchbacks with excellent views of the cove mark the final descent. Pass the Crooked Arm Cascade. At the junction, turn left to return to the road and your car.

This trail can be abundant in wildlife. We've seen deer, squirrels, chipmunks, and many, many, birds. In the fall, the leaf colors and overlooks are exceptional. Spring flowers are abundant, especially near Marthas Branch. Spend the whole day on this trail or combine it with the Cades Cove Loop Road.

38. SPENCE FIELD

10.6 miles roundtrip

Allow 7 to 8 hours

Older elementary schoolers and **teens** will be challenged by this moderate-to-strenuous walk that gains 3,000 feet in 5 miles. This hike offers the remnants of a grassy bald, scenic views, and spring flowers.

A Fed Bear Is a Dead Bear

Wild bears live on berries, nuts, other animals, plants, or almost anything. If they are fed by humans, even accidentally, the bears become accustomed to people. Some of the deadliest foods to a bear are peanut butter sandwiches, watermelons, apple cores, and fried chicken. When bears are fed these foods, they lose their fear of humans and can become dangerous. *Do not feed bears! Do not leave food or trash out for bears!* Dispose of your garbage in bear-proof containers or take it with you. Never leave a pack unattended or drop a pack for a bear to get them to leave you alone.

How to Get There: The trail begins at the upper level of Cades Cove Picnic Area, on the left as you enter Cades Cove. Restrooms are in the picnic area or at the amphitheater near the campground.

Description of the Hike: Begin on the Anthony Creek Trail, which is graveled. At 0.2 miles, the Crib Gap Trail comes in from the left. Walk through the horse camp site and stable area. Continue straight ahead on the horse trail. The Russell Field Trail leads to the right at 1.6 miles. (This trail goes 3.5 miles to the crest of the Smokies at Russell Field, which is 2.8 miles from Spence Field via the Appalachian Trail. A long 13.5-mile loop could be made. However, for families, it might be best to limit your sights to Spence Field.)

Continue to the left on the Anthony Creek Trail. The trail winds though large, dying hemlocks with patches of rosebay rhododendron. Trillium, mayapple, dwarf iris, foamflower, silver bell, and tulip tree provide a fine show in April and May. After crossing Anthony Creek for the second time at 2 miles, the trail becomes steeper as it ascends Bote Mountain.

You will reach the Bote Mountain Trail at 3.6 miles. This trail began in the 1830s as a road over the mountains built by Cherokee labor. The story is that a vote was taken as to which ridge the road should ascend. Bote Mountain won and Defeat Ridge lost. Since there is no *v* in the Cherokee language, everyone cast their *bote*. The road, never completed from the North Carolina side, was used by settlers to herd livestock to the grassy fields and to haul lumber from the forests.

Turn right onto the Bote Mountain Trail, which runs 1.7 miles to the crest. In early May, this is a beautiful stretch with many wildflowers. Large patches of spring beauty and yellow trout lily grow in profusion. When you reach Spence Field, the open places are beautiful! Spence Field was once a large grassy bald, but trees and shrubs are reclaiming the area. You will emerge at a junction with the Appalachian Trail (A.T.). The best views are to the left along the A.T. in small grassy areas. In these areas (4,890 feet above sea level), serviceberry trees (locally called *sarvis*) blossom in May. Fine views of North Carolina and Tennessee please the eye.

The A.T. makes good connections with Rocky Top and Thunderhead, which are 1.2 and 2 miles to the east, respectively, and with Russell Field 2.8 miles to the west. Just remember that Thunderhead is a 700-foot gain in elevation and will add 4 miles to the hike.

Allow plenty of time to enjoy the views from Spence Field. Because of abundant wildlife in nearby Cades Cove, we often spot deer, squirrels, skunks, and even a bear. Please remember—*Don't feed the wildlife!* It harms the animals and can harm you. The return trip is all downhill and fairly easy. You may be surprised at how quickly you can make the return trip.

39. ELIJAH OLIVER PLACE

1 mile roundtrip
Allow 1 to 1.5 hours

Elementary schoolers will enjoy this easy walk to an old house site with a barn and log buildings.

How to Get There: Take the Cades Cove Loop Road about 4.3 miles to a parking area on the left. The trailhead is across the road from the parking area.

Description of the Hike: Start across from the parking area and pass by a gate onto a gravel path. Look for the remnants of a root cellar on the right of the trail about 130 yards from the beginning, just after a slight rise. In the spring, you will notice daffodils around the old house site.

Beyond the house site, cross a footlog over a small stream. The Wet Bottom Trail comes in from the right. A large barn is 75 yards past the creek. Continue on the gravel roadbed. The Wet Bottom Trail splits to the left after the barn.

The barn at the Elijah Oliver place shows a way of life now gone.

This house was built by Elijah Oliver, son of John Oliver who built the cabin near the beginning of the Cades Cove Loop Road (see Hike #36 on page 78). Elijah was born in Cades Cove in 1824. Wander through all the buildings that housed the Olivers and their animals. Notice the large junipers that the Olivers planted near their house. This tree is not common in the Smokies and is often seen at old house sites.

There is a side trail that follows the branch down to Abrams Creek Trailhead about 0.5 miles away. It's fun to go down that trail and follow the Wet Bottom Trail back up. This adds about 1 mile to the walk.

Even young children will like the walk to the Elijah Oliver Place and will find it easy.

40. ABRAMS FALLS

5 miles roundtrip

Allow 3 hours

Elementary schoolers will enjoy this moderate walk that gains 400 feet in 2.5 miles. This hike offers a large waterfall, spring flowers, and an enjoyable walk along Abrams Creek.

How to Get There: Take the Cades Cove Loop Road about 5 miles to a right turn after crossing Abrams Creek. Follow the gravel road 0.5 miles to a parking area. There are pit toilets at the parking lot. Other restrooms are available at the Cable Mill Visitor Center (which includes a resource store) beyond the Abrams Falls Road.

Description of the Hike: Start at the parking area at the junction of Mill and Abrams Creeks. A footbridge crosses Abrams Creek to a trail split. To the right, it is 0.5 miles through bottomland to the Elijah Oliver house. This is an excellent walk for preschoolers and elementary schoolers to see a restored homesite. To the left is the Abrams Creek Trail, which goes through a rhododendron tunnel that is especially beautiful when in full bloom in late spring.

The trail generally follows the creek until it ascends a pine-covered ridge at about 0.5 miles. Cross Arbutus Branch before climbing Arbutus Ridge, 200 feet above the creek. At 1 mile, the trail reaches the ridgetop; then it descends through pine and mountain laurel. This area was damaged when an F4 tornado blasted through on April 27, 2011. The tornado cut a 13-mile-long and 0.25-mile-wide swath through the western end of Great Smoky Mountains National Park. The area is growing back, but downed trees and a cleared ridge side still show the devastation.

Historic structures, like Cable Mill in Cades Cove, abound in the park.

The trail crosses a footlog over Stony Branch. A third and final ridge is climbed at 2 miles. Do not give up! You are almost there! The last 0.2 miles down to Wilson Creek can be difficult for smaller children. Watch them closely. Cross a footlog over Wilson Creek at 2.5 miles. Closely supervise children while on the rocks around the falls.

The 25-foot-high Abrams Falls plunges into a large pool with the volume of water of a small river rather than a creek. Eighteen creeks and branches flow into Cades Cove to form Abrams Creek, which is the only water exit from the cove to the Little Tennessee River. Abrams Creek and Falls were probably named for Old Abraham, a Cherokee who lived near the cove in Chilhowee. A Cherokee village called *Tsiyahi*, Otter Place, was likely named for the otters who frolicked in the creek. In the early 1990s, river otters were reintroduced following a feasibility study conducted here on Abrams Creek.

Return to the parking lot by the same trail. This is a beautiful walk in the spring and summer providing plenty of wildflowers, rhododendron, and mountain laurel, as well as many opportunities for playing in the creek. This hike goes well with a day trip through Cades Cove. Picnic at the falls or at the Cable Mill Visitor Center. The Cades Cove Loop Road can be very crowded, especially in the summer and fall.

41. GREGORY BALD

11 miles roundtrip

Allow 6 to 8 hours

Older elementary schoolers and **teens** will be challenged by this difficult hike that gains 3,000 feet over 5.5 miles. This hike offers a grassy bald, spring flowers, and scenic views.

How to Get There: The trailhead for Gregory Ridge Trail is at a turnaround at the end of Forge Creek Road. Forge Creek Road branches off the Cades Cove Loop Road at the Cable Mill parking area. Follow Forge Creek Road approximately 2 miles to the intersection with Parsons Branch Road, which is now closed due to storm damage. The parking area and turnaround are just past this intersection.

Description of the Hike: The Gregory Ridge Trail begins along the east bank of Forge Creek. For the first 2 miles, the trail essentially follows Forge Creek through a pine and hemlock forest. The first mile has very

Otter

In the 1990s, the northern river otter was reintroduced to the Smokies in releases around the park. These furry animals often hunt at night in rivers and creeks. Otters build dens under logs, in river banks, in natural hollows, and in the abandoned burrows of other animals. Otter dens usually have an underwater entrance and are lined with bark, grass, leaves, and moss. The otters' webbed feet make them excellent swimmers and divers.

Otters weigh between 11 and 30 pounds and can be from 35 to 50 inches long. They live from 8 to 9 years in the wild, but some have lived up to 20 years in captivity. An otter can stay under water for nearly 8 minutes and can run up to 18 miles per hour on land.

Look for river otters along the larger creeks and rivers. They are most likely to be seen in early morning and just before dark. They are fun-loving creatures and will entertain you with their antics.

little elevation gain and is a cool, easy stretch padded with pine needles. At 0.25 miles from the trailhead, cross Forge Creek on a footlog. In the second mile, the trail begins a moderate climb as it rises away from the sound of Forge Creek below on the left. Large tulip trees are mixed with hemlock and rhododendron.

Just below Campsite #12, which is located two miles from the parking area, you will cross Forge Creek two more times on sturdy footlogs. Campsite #12 is a pleasant, open area under the canopy of large trees with several good tent sites. A walk to Campsite #12 and back to the parking area is a nice 4-mile hike. It is a good overnight hike for children who cannot travel long distances with a backpack.

To this point, you have followed an ancient aboriginal route over the mountains that was first used by elk, buffalo, deer, and other wildlife. At Campsite #12, the old trail leaves Forge Creek to the left and climbs to Ekaneetlee Gap. This trail is not maintained by the park. Be aware of this route that has crossed the Smokies for thousands of years.

After passing the campsite, the trail begins a steady climb up Gregory Ridge, leaving Forge Creek behind. The ridge crest is 0.6 miles above the campsite in a drier pine-oak forest. A few open places offer good views of the surrounding mountains. The trail follows the ridge, occasionally dipping below the crest on either side. Although the moderate climb is steady, the footing is good, making for easy walking. Galax lines much of the trail in this section and blooms in mid-to-late May.

Rich Gap and the Gregory Bald Trail are reached at 4.9 miles. At the junction, Gregory Bald Trail goes left for 2 miles to reach the Appalachian Trail (A.T.) at Doe Knob. Your route is to the right, where you will climb another 0.6 miles to Gregory Bald (4,950 feet above sea level).

This open bald is named for Russell Gregory (1795-1864) who settled in the Cades Cove area in the 1830s. Gregory loved the mountains, especially the balds. He hunted and herded on the bald that bears his name. Gregory built a cylindrical stone house with large openings for windows through which he shot deer and other game on clear moonlit nights. He had eight children, many of whom stayed in the area to raise their families. Confederate camp guards killed Gregory in the winter of 1864. His descendants were living in Cades Cove when it became part of the park in the 1930s.

Gregory Bald has an amazing display of flame azaleas. The variety of colors is overwhelming! The best time for the blooms is around the second or third week of June. From the large, grassy bald are good views of Cades Cove to the north and Fontana Lake and the North Carolina mountains to the south. The A.T. once crossed Gregory Bald but was rerouted after the completion of Fontana Dam in the 1940s.

Numerous blueberry bushes along the fringes of the bald can provide a tasty snack in late summer. The greenish-yellow knots about the size of a child's fist on flame azalea branches are azalea galls, which are watery inside and bitter to the taste. They were used as a source for water and as a medicinal herb. Lie in the grass and imagine the sound of cow bells,

White-Tailed Deer

Even though deer can often be seen in Cades Cove, about 6,000 deer live everywhere in the Smokies. Fawns are born between late May and early August. A fawn's only defense is a pattern of white spots on its back that helps it blend into its surroundings. Male deer, called bucks, begin growing antlers in spring of their second year. The antlers are fully developed in August and fall off in the winter. Deer browse on grass, leaves, and nuts.

the lowing of cattle, and the bleating of sheep that once summered on the cool mountain tops. Enjoy a picnic, look for monsters and animals in cloud shapes, or count imaginary sheep (take a nap).

The Cherokee called Gregory Bald *Tsistu'yi*, the Rabbit Place. It was believed that a great townhouse was in the bald's grasses where the Great Rabbit, chief of all rabbits, presided. In the old times, as it was told, humans could see the Great Rabbit who was larger than a deer. All rabbits were considered the Great Rabbit's subjects. Now people can see only the Great Rabbit's tribe and the grassy area where his townhouse once stood. Look closely in the shade around the fringe—perhaps you will see deer, rabbits, or other wildlife.

The origin of the grassy balds is not fully understood. They were in existence before the Cherokee lived in the region. However, the grazing of cattle, sheep, and hogs expanded the grassy areas, which the park service maintains so that all might enjoy them as Russell Gregory did over 100 years ago. Return to the parking area via the same route.

42. LOOK ROCK TOWER

1 mile roundtrip

Allow 30 minutes to 1 hour

Preschoolers and **elementary schoolers** will like this short walk to an observation tower with wonderful views of the Smokies and the Great Valley of the Tennessee River.

How to Get There: Take the Foothills Parkway 9.5 miles west from US 321 toward US 129. The parking lot is on the left.

Description of the Hike: This short walk starts across the road from the upper end of the parking lot. Walk the paved path up to the top of the ridge. About halfway up, the narrow trail turns left onto a paved roadbed. You will pass an air-quality monitoring station with wonderful views west and north.

At 0.5 miles, you reach the base of the observation tower. Walk up the ramp for a magnificent 360-degree view of the mountains. To the southeast are Gregory and Parsons Balds. Thunderhead and Clingmans Dome are in the distance to the east. Rich Mountain is in the foreground to the southeast. To the north and west is the Great Valley of the Tennessee. On

Night Life in the Smokies

Half of the time it is dark in the Smokies. Most people miss this part of the Smokies experience. Owls, whip-poor-wills, lightning bugs, glowworms, and more are out only at night. The fields of Cataloochee and Cades Cove offer wonderful views of the skies far from city lights. On a moonless night, the Milky Way arches high over the mountains in these dark places. Remember that it takes the human eye 30 minutes to fully adjust to darkness. Most families don't spend that much time in the dark. Find a spot with no artificial light to look, to listen, to experience the Smokies in a whole different way. After all, half of the park is after dark.

a clear day, the Cumberland Plateau is visible on the horizon. Poor air quality often reduces the visibility to less than 20 miles.

It is thought that Captain Juan Pardo and his soldiers camped near this spot in October 1567 as they moved through the area. They visited a village at the mouth of Abrams Creek about 8.5 miles to the west. Exhibits in Townsend and at the Great Smoky Mountains Heritage Center explain the history of American Indian life in the region over about 12,000 years.

The hike to Look Rock Tower is a great walk any time of year. The leaves in the fall provide an amazing display. The clear skies offer a good look at the stars and moon. Consider coming to Look Rock to watch the Perseid meteor shower in the second week of August. This is a nice, short walk with a good drive along the Foothills Parkway.

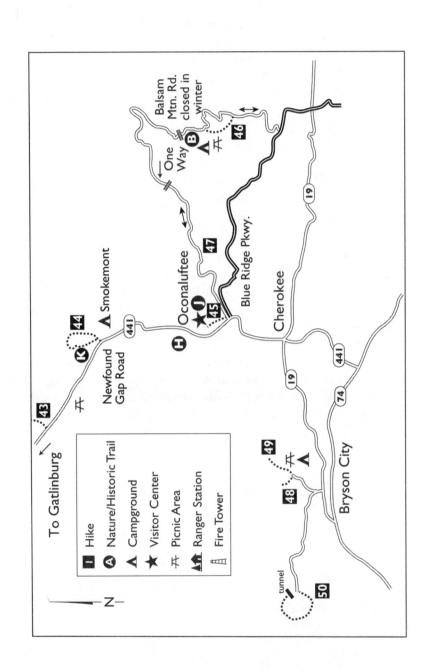

Cherokee–Deep Creek

Cherokee is on the park's southern boundary at the junction of US 441 and US 19, about 1.5 hours from Gatlinburg. It is in the Qualla Boundary, the home of the Eastern Band of Cherokee Indians. In the town of Cherokee are several opportunities to learn more about the American Indian inhabitants of the Smokies. The Oconaluftee Indian Village, the Cherokee Museum, and *Unto These Hills*, a nightly summer drama, are the best bets to learn about Cherokee life and history.

The Oconaluftee Visitor Center is at the southern entrance to the park on US 441 (Newfound Gap Road) near Cherokee. The Mountain Farm Homestead is a good interpretation of mountain life in the 1800s, as is nearby Mingus Mill. The southern terminus of the Blue Ridge Parkway is near the visitor center. This national parkway gives access to some of the most beautiful mountain scenery in the eastern United States.

National park campgrounds located near Cherokee are Smokemont (on US 441, 3.2 miles north of the visitor center), Balsam Mountain (9 miles off the Blue Ridge Parkway), and Deep Creek (near Bryson City). These three campgrounds usually are not as crowded as those on the Tennessee side.

The Deep Creek campground is located north of Bryson City on Deep Creek. Take US 19 south 10 miles from Cherokee to Bryson City. Turn onto Everett Street in Bryson City. At 0.2 miles, turn right onto Depot Street, then turn left onto Ramseur Street. After another immediate turn to the right, the road becomes curvy. Follow the signs to the Deep Creek Campground, which is 4 miles from Bryson City. Tubing is very popular in the Deep Creek area in the summer. The campground and parking areas can be crowded in the summer months.

Lake View Drive (also known as the Road to Nowhere) and the tunnel can be reached by staying on Everett Street in Bryson City. The road goes into the park and dead-ends at the tunnel about 8 miles from Bryson City.

Cherokee and Bryson City are the quieter side of the Smokies, although the casino in Cherokee has increased its popularity. The south side of the park provides many opportunities for fun with the whole family. In addition to the hikes, other diversions are: tubing, museums, drama, and a train ride to Dillsboro on the Great Smoky Mountains Railroad. Enjoy this area that is little used and often forgotten.

43. KEPHART PRONG

4 miles roundtrip

Allow 3.5 to 4 hours

Elementary schoolers and older children will enjoy this moderate walk that gains 800 feet in 2 miles. This hike offers historical sites, a creek, and a shelter for an overnight stay.

How to Get There: The trailhead is 7.1 miles north of the Oconaluftee Visitor Center on US 441 (8.8 miles south of Newfound Gap). Park at the pull-off along the Oconaluftee River, 15 minutes from Cherokee and 1 hour from Gatlinburg. The nearest restrooms are at Collins Creek Picnic Area (2 miles toward Cherokee), at Smokemont Campground, and at Oconaluftee Visitor Center.

Description of the Hike: This hike can be an overnight outing for older elementary schoolers who are beginning to have a sense of history. Many elements of the Smokies' history are present along this trail: the Cherokee, lumber company logging, and New Deal conservation.

Kephart Prong and Mt. Kephart are named for Horace Kephart (1862–1931). He was a noted outdoorsman and author of *Camping and Woodcraft* and *Our Southern Highlanders*, both classics in the fields of camping and Appalachian studies. Kephart wrote extensively in support of establishing a national park in the Smokies.

Begin the hike by crossing a bridge over the Oconaluftee River. Oconaluftee is the Cherokee word for "by the river" and was applied to several villages in this valley. A low stone wall on the other side of the river was part of a Civilian Conservation Corps (CCC) camp. A stone sign and chimney on the right mark the entrance of the old camp. The boxwoods at the entrance are reminders of the gateway that once stood there. Beyond the CCC camp, when the trail divides, take the left fork across the creek on a footlog. Underfoot are pieces of pavement that are the remnants of an old road.

The forest here is typical second growth that follows logging operations. It is predominantly tulip tree with a generous understory of rhododendron. An old cistern is on the steep hillside to the left. It may be difficult to spot with all the undergrowth. A railroad bed that was first used in 1917 by the Champion Fibre Company to log this area is now the path. Keep an eye out for rails and cable scattered on the trail. At 0.75 miles, the trail recrosses the creek on a footlog.

One quarter mile farther, a little detour off the old roadbed goes through some beautiful dwarf iris that blooms in the spring. Cross a third footlog before rejoining the railroad bed. The trail gets rockier but not too difficult. Recross Kephart Prong on a fourth footlog just before reaching the Kephart Prong Shelter, which sleeps 12, at 2 miles. Stay the night on its wooden bunks and listen to Kephart Prong; return the next morning by the same route. Located in a wooded spot with the sound of rushing water as a lullaby, this shelter is a nice resting spot. Reservations must be made for the use of the shelter through the park's Backcountry Information Office. Notice the cable systems for hanging food away from bears.

Kephart Prong Trail is most enjoyable in the spring when the wildflowers are in bloom or in the fall when the leaves are in brilliant colors. Two trails continue up to the Appalachian Trail from the shelter: the Grassy Branch Trail (3.7 miles) and the Sweat Heifer Trail (3.6 miles). The elevation gain on each is over 2,000 feet, so be prepared for a steep climb! Kephart Prong Trail brings to mind why Horace Kephart worked so diligently to preserve this area.

44. SMOKEMONT LOOP

3.4 miles or 6 miles roundtrip

Allow 2 or 4 hours

Preschoolers and older children will enjoy the easy, shorter hike. The longer hike is moderate and appropriate for **elementary schoolers** and older. The shorter hike has only a small gain in elevation in 1.7 miles; while the longer hike gains 1,200 feet in 3.5 miles. These hikes offer creeks, spring and summer flowers, and fall colors.

How to Get There: The trailhead is in the upper end of the Smokemont Campground, 3.2 miles north of the Oconaluftee Visitor Center off the Newfound Gap Road (US 441). Restrooms are available in the campground.

Description of The Hike: The first leg of the hike is on the Bradley Fork Trail, which is a multiple-use trail. The stream is an enjoyable one in which children can wade and play. Its music is easily heard from the many benches along this gentle stretch. After about 0.5 miles is an old house site, easily identified by boxwoods that grow to the right of the old roadbed.

After the junction with the Chasteen Creek Trail, the trail climbs through rhododendron. At 1.7 miles, the Smokemont Loop goes to the left while the Bradley Fork Trail continues straight ahead. Families with younger children may wish to turn around and return by the same route for a shorter 3.4-mile walk.

Older children will be challenged by the next few miles. The trail crosses two narrow footlogs. The first is long and high above the creek. After the second log, the trail turns to the right and goes 1 mile up Richland Mountain. Views of Becks Bald to the east combined with many wildflowers—such as galax, mountain laurel, asters, closed gentian, and various ferns, including the beautiful maiden hair fern—make a scenic walk. In the fall, the many hardwoods produce colorful leaves.

After the trail crosses the ridge, the Oconaluftee River and Thomas Divide are to the west. At the trail's highest point, 4 miles from the trailhead, a large log offers a nice resting spot. Numerous downed chestnuts provide an opportunity to talk about the chestnut blight that plagued the area in the early 1900s. Dead and dying hemlocks offer a modern-day example of an exotic insect's invasion.

Beside the trail are some little brown jug plants. In addition to the unusual brown "flowers" that bloom in May, the leaves are very fragrant. It is said that children once pressed the aromatic leaves in their schoolbooks or kept them in their lunch pails.

Less than a mile from the end of the trail is the Bradley Cemetery. It shares the name of the family for whom the stream at the beginning of the hike was named. Rubbings with paper and charcoal can be made of the tombstones. The trail descends to the Oconaluftee River. You will recross Bradley Fork on a concrete bridge, built in 1921, above its junction with the Oconaluftee. Enter the campground on the south end and walk through it to the starting point.

Plan to play in the creeks. These are good hikes in the spring (wildflowers), fall (leaves and views), or summer (cool creek and flowers). The Smokemont Nature Trail is a good addition to a day in the area.

45. OCONALUFTEE CHEROKEE (BILINGUAL)

4 miles roundtrip

Allow 1.5 to 2 hours

Preschoolers and **elementary schoolers** will enjoy this walk through the Mountain Farm Museum and along the Oconaluftee River from the visitor center in the land of the Cherokee.

How to Get There: Begin at the Oconaluftee Visitor Center 2 miles inside the park from Cherokee, North Carolina. Walk through the Mountain Farm Museum; the trailhead is on the downstream end of the small farm homestead.

Description of the Hike: The first part of the walk is through the Mountain Farm Museum. The buildings here are authentic from the late 1800s and early 1900s but come from various locations throughout the park. Allow children plenty of time to explore.

This trail follows the Oconaluftee River from the visitor center to the town of Cherokee. Signs along the trail, which are in English and Cherokee, tell of the importance of mountains and the river through artwork and stories. This is a wonderful way to talk about other people, times, and cultures.

Throw rocks in the stream as you go along. Rhododendron is abundant on this walk. Elk often graze in the fields around the Oconaluftee Visitor Center. You will pass under the southern terminus of the Blue Ridge Parkway, a 470-mile-long adventure that connects Great Smoky Mountains National Park to Shenandoah National Park in Virginia.

A New Written Language

Sikwa'yi, Sequoyah, was born in Tuskegee town, near the old Fort Loudoun around 1760. With no proper education or familiarity with the English alphabet, he developed a Cherokee syllabary, which was quickly adopted by the entire Cherokee nation. Within a matter of a few years, many Cherokee could read and write the Cherokee language.

46. FLAT CREEK

5.2 miles roundtrip

Allow 3 hours

Elementary schoolers will like this moderate, high-elevation hike that offers a creek, waterfall, scenic views, spring flowers, and fall colors.

How to Get There: Take the Blue Ridge Parkway, just south of Oconaluftee Visitor Center. At Milepost 458 on the Blue Ridge Parkway, turn onto Heintooga Ridge Road, which will take you into the Great Smoky Mountains National Park. About 5 miles after leaving the Blue Ridge Parkway, you will find a small parking lot and the trailhead on your left.

Description of the Hike: The trailhead for Flat Creek Trail begins at the parking lot and descends a slightly steep grade. There are some logs on the trail to form steps. Along the way you will encounter creek crossings either on footlogs or by rock hopping. After crossing Bunches Creek, you will begin a steeper climb and eventually see Flat Creek to your left.

Flat Creek Falls is down in the trees and mountain laurel. It is difficult to see the entirety of this beautiful waterfall that splashes more than 200 feet off the side of Balsam Mountain. In the early spring and late fall, when the leaves are off the trees, there are views of the falls from the road near where your car is parked.

As you climb, you will begin to see grass growing alongside the trail. The grass becomes heavier until large areas of the forest are literally covered in this tall grass. The grass is evidence of extensive logging in the early 1900s. This is unusual, as you do not normally see areas of thick grass in the Smokies' forests.

As you near the end of the trail, you will join a nature trail that surrounds the Heintooga Picnic Area and the Balsam Mountain Campground. Along the trail is a water fountain and a bench with an awesome view north into the park. The Flat Creek Trail runs from the trailhead where you started to the end of the Heintooga Ridge Road.

The Heintooga Picnic Area is beautiful. Notice some of the picnic tables built from stone slabs. Restrooms are also available at the picnic area.

At this point, you can return to your car on the same trail, or take the 3.7-mile walk along the road back to your car. We enjoy a picnic at Heintooga Overlook or an overnight stay at the campground, the highest in the park at over 1 mile above sea level. Late June is a beautiful time to visit this higher-elevation area for its show of rhododendron, mountain laurel, flame azalea, and blackberries. Drive back to Cherokee on the 8.4-mile, one-way Heintooga Road down to Round Bottom Road, or via the Blue Ridge Parkway.

Note: Balsam Mountain Road is closed in the winter due to snow and ice at this elevation. Spring, fall, and summer are great on Balsam Mountain.

47. MINGO FALLS

0.5 miles roundtrip

Allow 30-45 minutes

Preschoolers and **elementary schoolers** can make this moderate walk to a magnificent waterfall.

How to Get There: Take Big Cove Road, which begins 1.5 miles south of the Oconaluftee Visitor Center. This road turns off Newfound Gap Road (US 441). Drive on Big Cove Road under the Blue Ridge Parkway 5 miles to the Mingo Falls Campground on the right. Cross the bridge to the campground. Parking is available to hikers. Remember this location is not in the national park but on private property. The nearest public restrooms are at the Oconaluftee Visitor Center.

Description of Hike: The wide trail begins to the left of the water plant for the campground. Ascend the steps for the first 200 yards; then the trail levels off to follow the creek around the ridge to the base of the falls.

Mingo Falls lies outside the boundaries of the park within the Qualla Boundary. The ancestors of the Eastern Band of Cherokee Indians moved into the mountains to escape removal from their home territory in 1838. Many Cherokee hid in the inaccessible reaches of the Smokies to avoid forcible removal to what is now Oklahoma. This removal was called the Trail of Tears because nearly one fourth of the Cherokee nation died on the journey. The Qualla Boundary was established for those left in the mountainous region.

The water of Mingo Creek drops 180 feet over a bare metasandstone face along the Greenbrier Fault, one of the major fault lines through the Smokies. Point out the highly stratified rock to children and explain how the sediment of an ancient ocean formed these stones. Stand on the small bridge near the base of the falls for the best views. The return to your car is quick and easy.

The Cherokee call this waterfall Big Bear Falls. It is truly a beautiful sight.

Tsali

During the dark time of history known as the Cherokee Removal that resulted in the Trail of Tears, the Cherokee people were horribly mistreated. As one group of Cherokee was being moved, soldiers began prodding women and children with bayonets to move them. Tsali, an older man, could not bear to see his family treated in this manner. He, his three sons, his brother, and their families attempted an escape. In the resulting scuffle two soldiers were killed. Tsali and his small band escaped to the safety of the Smokies where they hid in a cave on the headwaters of Deep Creek.

Scholars disagree on exactly what happened next. One version is that Colonel Winfield Scott, who supervised the removal for the military, knew that it would be difficult for his soldiers to go into the mountains to retrieve this band and the many other Cherokee who had fled. He offered a compromise through W.H. (Will) Thomas, a friend and confidant of the Cherokee. If Tsali and his family would surrender to the army, some of the escaped Cherokee would be allowed to stay in the mountains until their fate was decided by Congress.

Tsali, upon hearing the offer, voluntarily went to Colonel Scott's headquarters. Tsali and two of his sons were shot by a firing squad. The third son was spared due to his young age. The firing squad was made up of Cherokee prisoners who were forced to participate to show their "utter helplessness."

Tsali's sacrifice made it possible for what became the Eastern Band of Cherokee Indians to remain in the Smokies.

48. JUNEY WHANK FALLS

0.6 miles roundtrip

Allow 1 hour

Preschoolers can walk this easy trail that gains 200 feet in 0.3 miles. This hike features a waterfall and a creek.

How to Get There: The trail begins at a parking area that is 0.4 miles past the entrance to the Deep Creek Picnic Area. Restrooms are available in the picnic area and campground. The picnic area is open year-round; the campground is seasonal.

Description of the Hike: The trail is somewhat steep at first but is worth the effort. It leads through a hardwood forest where it's fun to listen to the birds. A side trail at 0.3 miles leads to a footbridge with a bench. The bridge is located at the halfway point along the 80-foot falls, with about 40 feet of waterfall above the bridge and about the same below. Here you can experience the sight, feel, and sound of the waterfall.

Continue across the footbridge to a trail junction. A left turn will take you on a short loop above Juney Whank Falls and then return downhill to the parking area. A right turn will take you to the Deep Creek Trail for an easy 0.2-mile walk to Toms Branch Falls. Indian Creek Falls is 0.7 miles up the trail (see Hike #49 below).

Juney Whank is a wonderful, short hike that fits well with an overnight stay at Deep Creek Campground, a hike to Indian Creek Falls or Toms Branch Falls, and/or tubing on Deep Creek. There are vendors for tubing equipment located outside the park. The Deep Creek area is a true Smoky Mountain treasure. In summer, especially on the weekends, the area can be very popular. It is most fun on hot days when the cool creeks and falls are inviting.

49. INDIAN CREEK FALLS

2 miles roundtrip

Allow 2 hours

Preschoolers and **elementary schoolers** will like this easy hike to beautiful waterfalls.

How to Get There: The trail begins at a parking area 0.4 miles past the entrance to the Deep Creek Picnic Area. Restrooms are available in the picnic area and campground. The picnic area is open year-round; the campground is seasonal.

Description of the Hike: Leave the parking area on the Deep Creek Trail, a multiple-use trail popular with horseback riders and tubers. It is an easy walk beside Deep Creek, which is wonderful for tubing, wading, or swimming in the hottest summer months. Children can safely run ahead while remaining in sight. Toms Branch Falls is on the opposite side of Deep Creek, 0.25 miles from the parking area. Springtime, when the water is plentiful and the leaves are few, brings out the beauty in this cascade.

The leaves are colorful during autumn in this second-growth forest of pine and oak. Spring wildflowers—fire pink, mountain laurel, rhododendron, and jack-in-the-pulpit to name only a few—are abundant in this moist clime of the Smokies. Take time to play in Deep Creek. Crayfish (crawdads), trout, water spiders, and salamanders are plentiful enough for young eyes to spot quickly. Sometimes it is fun to mark off a small area and see how many life forms can be found.

You will cross Deep Creek on a wide bridge, which is a wonderful place to throw rocks and sticks into the swift current. At the trail divide

Salamanders

Mountain people called these amphibians "spring lizards." Although not related to lizards, salamanders are all over the Smokies. In fact, the park is known as the Salamander Capital of the World, with over 30 species, some found *only* in the Smokies. Most species are "lungless" meaning they "breathe" through their skin and the linings of their mouths and throats. Salamanders live under rocks and logs along and in streams. Do not pick up salamanders; just look at them. Also, do not rearrange logs and rocks to find salamanders. Would you want someone to lift the roof off your house and stare at you?

Ocoee salamander, Jordan's salamander, Santeetlah dusky salamander, Blue Ridge spring salamander, and shovelnose salamander are names of only a few. The eastern hellbender can grow to be two feet long!

(0.9 miles), take the right fork on Indian Creek Trail, an old jeep road. After a few hundred yards, follow the small trail on the left. Descend to a large pool at the base of 60-foot Indian Creek Falls. Rhododendron blooms frame the falls in June.

Take your time on this easy hike and plan to get wet. Wear old tennis shoes, sandals, or water shoes so that wading will be safe and fun (but have a dry pair at the car.) The walk to Juney Whank Falls is nearby. Riding on the Great Smoky Mountain Railroad, tubing the creek, and camping in Deep Creek Campground are all great complements to Indian Creek Falls.

50. GOLDMINE LOOP

3 miles roundtrip

Allow 1.5 to 2 hours

Elementary schoolers can make this moderate hike to an old farm site and campsite.

How to Get There: From the intersection of US 441 and US 19 in Cherokee, North Carolina, drive south on US 19 for 9 miles to Bryson City. In Bryson City, turn right onto Everett Street. Drive on Everett Street for 3 miles to the Great Smoky Mountains Park entrance. Continue for 6 miles to the parking area at the end of Lakeview Drive.

The last 6 miles of this drive are known as "the Road to Nowhere." When Fontana Dam was built during World War II, the impounded waters of the Little Tennessee River flooded NC Route 288. A promise was made to build a road from Bryson City to Fontana Dam. This road was started in 1960. After the first 6 miles and the tunnel were constructed, the project was canceled due to budget and environmental problems. Local people called the broken promise—the Road to Nowhere. Now it serves as a wonderful place to take you to Nowhere.

Description of the Hike: Reach the Goldmine Loop Trail by walking through the tunnel where the Lakeshore Trail begins. The tunnel is level and an easy walk, but you may want to bring a flashlight; it can be very dark, even on a sunny day, or when returning late in the day. The tunnel is 1,200-feet long. Once through the tunnel, continue walking on the roadway, which eventually becomes a dirt trail.

Roughly 0.6 miles from the parking lot, you will reach the Tunnel Bypass Trail. This trail is used by hikers and horseback riders to avoid walking through the tunnel. Continue on the Lakeshore Trail another 0.1 miles to the Goldmine Loop Trail on the left.

The trail descends steeply through mountain laurel and holly. At a saddle in the ridge, the trail moderates and descends to an old farm site. The trail bears to the left to skirt a clearing.

At 0.3 miles, the remnants of a chimney are on the right. Other signs of the old farm are scattered about—cans, bottles, crockery, glass, and tubs. A small stream separates the trail from the old house site.

The trail follows an old roadbed and Goldmine Branch, which flows down to Fontana Lake. On the right at 0.75 miles, another house site can be seen across Goldmine Branch. Two large boxwoods, steps, and a rock-lined cellar remain.

The trail goes left away from the old road for a few hundred yards. At 0.9 miles, a path on the left leaves the trail to follow Hyatt Branch 300 yards to Campsite #67. An old chimney and stone piles are the remains of a house and farm that belonged to Elias Hyatt.

Back at the main trail, continue down Goldmine Branch to where it joins the lake. Circle the water, cross a small branch, and follow Tunnel Branch steeply up the side of the ridge. At a level area, the trail turns left and continues the ascent. At 2 miles from the trailhead, you will reach a junction with the Tunnel Bypass Trail. To the left, it is 1.8 miles back to the car through the tunnel. However, continue ahead 0.4 miles to the parking area. This can be a wet, mucky trail in rainy times.

A Cherokee legend said that Cherokee hid gold in a cave or tunnel, but it appears there was no gold mine in this area. There was limited mining in the general area, mostly to the east at Eagle Creek.

Fontana

Fontana Village is a resort area that was developed from the housing built for the construction workers of Fontana Dam. Follow US 129 from the Foothills Parkway or Maryville to NC 28 at Deals Gap. From there, turn onto NC 28 and drive 11 miles to Fontana. Beautiful overlooks are on US 129 and NC 28. It is a 24-mile drive from the intersection of US 129 and the Foothills Parkway to Fontana Village. From Cherokee, take US 19 through Bryson City until it intersects NC 28, which goes to Fontana.

Fontana Dam, the highest dam in the Tennessee Valley Authority system at 480 feet, was built during World War II to supply Oak Ridge and Alcoa with electric power. The Appalachian Trail passes over the dam on its way into the national park. The Fontana area is one of the quieter spots in the Smokies, attracting many fishermen to the lake and creeks. Restrooms and a picnic area are located at Fontana Dam.

51. TWENTYMILE CREEK CASCADE

1.25 miles roundtrip

Allow 1 to 1.5 hours

Preschoolers and **elementary schoolers** can make this easy walk to a pretty cascade amid rhododendron.

How to Get There: Go to the Twentymile Ranger Station on NC 28, which is 3 miles east of the junction with US 129 at Deals Gap and 6.2 miles west of Fontana Dam. The junction of the west end of the Foothills Parkway and US 129 is 18.5 miles away. Parking areas are located above and below the ranger station. The nearest public restrooms are at the store at Deals Gap or in Fontana.

Description of the Hike: Begin at the ranger station on an old roadbed that climbs easily beside Twentymile Creek. The origin of this creek's name is a bit obscure. Some say that it was thought to be twenty miles downstream from the mouth of Hazel Creek. Others say it drained

Look Rock

Foothills
Pkwy.

42

N

Abrams Creek

Cades Cove

129

Parsons Branch

51

52

129

28

Fontana Village

Fontana
Lake

Hike

Nature/Historic Trail

Campground

Visitor Center

Picnic Area

Ranger Station

Fire Tower

*Parsons Branch currently closed

twenty miles of the mountains. Still others hold that it is twenty miles from the junction of the Little Tennessee River with the Tennessee River.

Twentymile is a secluded spot in the park that is well known to horseback riders. The trail is wide and easy to walk. Go 0.4 miles to a trail junction. Twentymile Creek and Moore Springs Branch come together where Wolf Ridge Trail joins the Twentymile Creek Trail. Cross the bridge and bear to the right. It is 100 yards up a slight grade to a small sign marking the side trail down to Twentymile Creek Cascade. The side trail descends a couple of switchbacks.

The metamorphic sandstone over which the water falls is criss-crossed with streaks of white quartz. The resulting cascades are pleasant. This is a good spot for a picnic or just for a rest on the long drive between Maryville and Fontana Village. In the spring, wildflowers are plentiful. The return to your car is by the same route.

52. SHUCKSTACK FIRE TOWER

7 miles roundtrip

Allow 6 hours

Older elementary schoolers and **teens** will find this strenuous hike a challenge as they climb 2,120 feet over 3.5 miles. This hike features a fire tower, scenic views, and fall colors.

How to Get There: Follow the signs to the Fontana Dam Visitor Center 3 miles past Fontana Village. Cross the dam to a parking area 0.5 miles past the dam. Restrooms are at the visitor center. If the road over the dam is closed to vehicles, remember that this will add 2 miles to the roundtrip mileage.

Description of the Hike: Follow the white blazes of the Appalachian Trail (A.T.) up Shuckstack Ridge. There is no notice of the Shuckstack Fire Tower on the trail sign. A series of switchbacks ascends through second-growth forest. The trail moderates after 2 miles, where the climb becomes less difficult but steady. For hikers who are walking the entire length of the A.T. (usually from south to north), this section is their first

Nature's many offerings entertain children.

taste of the Smokies, which are higher and more rugged than other sections in the South.

At 2.5 miles, the gap between Shuckstack and Little Shuckstack is reached. Beyond this is an overlook to the south with views of the Snowbird Mountains. The last 0.5 miles of the hike climbs to the top of Shuckstack Ridge. The fire tower is up a short, steep side trail (that is also not signed).

Some of the best views in the Smokies are from the fire tower. Fontana Dam is below, with Gregory Bald, Russell and Spence Fields, and Thunderhead to the north. High Rocks is beyond Eagle and Hazel Creeks to the east. To the south are the Yellow Creek and Cheoah Mountains, with the nearby Joyce Kilmer and Slickrock Wilderness Area to the southwest. A chimney and cistern, remnants of the log cabin where the lookout lived during fire season, are at the base of the tower. The 60-foot steel tower was built in 1935 and was used for the two fire seasons each year until 1968, when all the fire towers in the Smokies were decommissioned. This is one of only five remaining towers in the Smokies.

The downhill return trip is not difficult. However, take care—at certain times of the year, leaves and roots can make the trail slippery. A longer hike is possible on the Lost Cove and Lakeshore Trails (about 9 miles to the parking lot). This hike is difficult and wet (with many creek crossings) and should be undertaken only with teens who are up to a challenge. The Lost Cove Trail turns off the A.T. past the fire tower.

Nature and Historical Trails

Numerous nature and historical trails wind throughout the park. Brochures, which are available at the trailheads for a small charge, point out interesting features. These trails are suited for all ages. We like them because they are good for young children. Most are short and easy with plenty to see. One way we make them more enjoyable is to let the children read the brochures at the appropriate spot along the way. Below is a description of the location and highlights of the trails.

A. **Alum Cave Bluffs**—5 miles—Begins on Newfound Gap Road (US 441) 8.6 miles south of Sugarlands Visitor Center or 4.3 miles north of Newfound Gap. For a detailed description, see Hike #21 on page 42. This is an extremely popular hike, and the trail and parking lot can be crowded. Arrive early in the day or go during the winter or off-season.

B. **Balsam Mountain**—1 mile—Begins at the Balsam Mountain Campground 19 miles from Cherokee (9 miles off the Blue Ridge Parkway). An introduction to life one mile above sea level.

C. **Pine–Oak Trail**—1.5 miles—Begins at the Cades Cove Parking Area, at the store across from the ranger station. Walk 0.25 miles through the group campground to the trailhead. The 1-mile loop is a good introduction to the different trees of the Smokies and their uses by Cherokees and Euro-American settlers.

D. **Cosby**—1 mile—Begins at the amphitheater in the Cosby Campground about 20 miles east of Gatlinburg on US 321. Cross 10 footlogs over a small creek to explore stone fences and old house sites.

E. **Cove Hardwood**—0.75 miles—Begins at the entrance to the Chimneys Picnic Area, which is 4.5 miles from Sugarlands

Visitor Center on US 441. A variety of trees and plants can
be seen in this accessible and popular area. A good introduction to the forest of the Smokies is provided.

F. **Elkmont**—0.8 miles—Begins opposite the Elkmont Campground at a small parking area. An introductory lesson in
"reading the landscape" is fun for elementary schoolchildren
who can observe the forest.

G. **Laurel Falls**—2.5 miles—Begins at Fighting Creek Gap
on Little River Road between Gatlinburg and Townsend.
Parking is 3.8 miles from Sugarlands Visitor Center and 14
miles from Townsend. For details of the trail, see Hike #22
on page 50. This is an extremely popular hike, and the trail
and parking lot can be crowded. Arrive early in the day or go
during the winter or off-season.

H. **Mingus Mill**—0.5 miles—Begins 0.5 miles north of the
Oconaluftee Visitor Center off Newfound Gap Road (US
441). Restrooms are available at the parking lot. A turbine
mill, built in 1886, is in operation on the site of one originally
built in the 1700s. Watch grain being ground to meal and
flour at this living history demonstration. Walk beyond the
mill, past the flume, to a jeep road, which circles back to the
parking area. The demonstrations are seasonal, so check at
the Oconaluftee Visitor Center.

I. **Noah "Bud" Ogle Place**—0.75 miles—Begins on the Cherokee Orchard Road outside of Gatlinburg. Turn off US 441
onto Airport Road at traffic light #8, then drive 2.7 miles
to a parking area. A log house, barn, and tub mill are good
introductions to life in the Smokies. One of our favorites!

J. **Mountain Farm Museum**—0.25 miles—Located at the
Oconaluftee Visitor Center north of Cherokee. This historical demonstration allows your family to participate in the
life of a nineteenth century farm.

K. **Smokemont**—0.75 miles—Begins in the Smokemont Campground off Newfound Gap Road (US 441) 3.2 miles north of

the Oconaluftee Visitor Center. Explore the diverse vegetation and logging history.

L. **Spruce/Fir**—0.25 miles—Begins on the Clingmans Dome Road about 3 miles from Newfound Gap Road (US 441). This trail introduces the spruce-fir forest, which is not found farther south than the Smokies. Many of the spruce-fir trees are under attack from the balsam woolly adelgid.

M. **Fighting Creek**—1 mile—Begins behind the Sugarlands Visitor Center south of Gatlinburg on Newfound Gap Road (US 441). The trail includes a log cabin, creek, rhododendron, and second-growth forest. A good trail in combination with the exhibits in the visitor center. A side trail leads to Cataract Falls—see Hike #15 on page 32 for details.

N. **Sugarlands Valley All-Access Trail**—0.5 miles—A concrete path designed for persons with disabilities or young children in strollers. The interpretive signs are in relief and Braille. See Hike #13 on page 30 for details.

APPENDIX 2

Car Travel and Auto Tours

The best way to get a feel for the Smokies is to walk along the trails, to wade the creeks, and to peer through the bluish haze at the distant horizon. However, getting to these experiences means a ride in a car. Riding can sometimes be the most difficult part of the trip. We've done many things to make the drive easier and to pass the time. The following are our best suggestions, which were born in desperate moments.

A. **The License Plate Game**—This old standby is wonderful in the most visited national park in the US. Simply list the states and Canadian provinces you see. One afternoon we saw 35 states!

B. **Looking Contests**—Offer a small prize or reward for the one who sees the first deer, bear, flower, tree, etc. A variation is to keep a total of things observed. This is good in Cades Cove because the wildlife is abundant.

C. **Bingo**—Make up bingo cards with things that will be seen along the way. As the child sees the object, she puts an X on the square.

D. **Sing**—You don't have to be an opera or rock star for this to be fun. Standards for this area are: "On Top of Old Smoky," "She'll Be Comin' Round the Mountain," "I've Been Working on the Railroad," "Old McDonald Had a Farm," etc.

E. **Storytelling**—Tell stories from your own childhood, tell stories from the mountains or the Cherokee (see Resources on page 125), or make up stories as a family. Make up a story using your own children as characters in the Smokies. Another way to make up a story is with a stone that is passed from one person to another. The person with the stone gets to add the next sentence or two to the story.

F. **Read**—Pick out a good book to read a little at a time. Keep your audience hanging. This is a good way to introduce your children to some classics. Read some of the National Park literature, and allow others in the car to take turns reading. On the self-guided auto tours, let the children do the reading.

G. **Listen to Music, Stories, Books**—Try anything that your children enjoy listening to. Some parents allow each child to have their own personal listening device. This allows the child to listen to whatever he wishes.

H. **Games**—Many popular games have car editions. Also, card games are fun and easy to play.

I. **Maps**—Older children enjoy reading maps. Give children their own maps. Allow them to navigate by giving directions, or simply let them tell where the car is at the moment.

J. **When All Else Fails**—Simply Stop. Pull off at a scenic overlook, alongside a creek or river, at a Quiet Walkway, or almost anyplace. Get out of the car! Even if the kids don't calm down, you'll feel better and will be more patient.

Nothing works every time. No method is foolproof. Help them enjoy being together with you in the car. Try having a special bag or box of tricks. String them along for as long as you can.

Remember what it was like to travel when you were a child. Your concept of a short ride and your child's are very different. Sit in different seats occasionally. The adults don't always have to sit up front. (Also, parents should take turns driving. This prevents the same parent from always having to be the disciplinarian or the navigator.) Simply put, try not to overdo it. Make the car a place for Time Well Spent.

SELF-GUIDED AUTO TOURS

Self-guided auto tours are available in the park. These are through scenic areas with historical interest. We've enjoyed all of them because numerous stops provide plenty of occasions to romp, learn, and play. Booklets are available at the beginning of each tour for a small charge.

Cades Cove—Seven miles from the Townsend Y, the 11-mile loop shows life in a mountain community with cabins, houses, churches, cemeteries, and a mill. The Cades Cove Visitor Center is halfway around the loop at the Cable Mill area. Two roads (Sparks and Hyatt Lanes) allow the one-way loop to be shortened, while the Rich Mountain Road is a one-way exit. The Rich Mountain Road goes from the Missionary Baptist Church to Townsend and offers views of Cades Cove from the slopes of Rich Mountain. The Cades Cove Auto Tour can be very crowded and slow at times.

Abundant wildlife lives in Cades Cove and can be easily seen from the car. Deer, wild turkey, ground hog, fox, coyote, and bear are some of the animals in the cove. The best times for animal watching are just after sunrise and shortly before sunset. The campground and picnic area in Cades Cove provide many services. Horseback riding and bicycling are also available. In the summer, the Cades Cove Loop Road is closed to motor vehicles on Wednesdays for bicycling and walking. The road closes at sunset each day.

Cataloochee—Although a challenge to reach, it's worth the time and effort to visit this hidden treasure. Exit I-40 at US 276 (Exit 20—Maggie Valley in North Carolina). Turn onto Cove Creek Road after the interstate exit. The paved road becomes gravel near the top of the ridge but returns to pavement after 7.5 miles, once inside the park boundary. The 11 miles from the interstate to Cataloochee is a scenic drive. The valley was once a thriving community with over 1,200 people. It now contains several historic buildings, a campground, hiking and horseback riding trails, and plenty of wildlife—including elk! We've never been to Cataloochee when there were many people, so don't tell anyone about this jewel. We suggest you review the cautions in this guide and given by the National Park Service about viewing wildlife, especially elk, when venturing into Cataloochee.

Roaring Fork—To reach Roaring Fork, turn left off US 441 in Gatlinburg at traffic light #8 onto Historic Nature Trail/Airport Road. At the intersection below the Park Vista Hotel, bear right onto Cherokee Orchard Road. Follow this road into the park, past the Noah "Bud" Ogle Nature Trail, 3.7 miles to where the auto tour begins on the right. The 5.5-mile auto tour is paved but narrow and winding, forcing you to take it slow and easy. This is a one-way route that will take you to US 321 on the east side of Gatlinburg. It is closed in the winter but enjoyable in the other seasons.

Tremont Logging History—Turn off Laurel Creek Road beyond its intersection with Little River Road (at the Townsend Y) and drive 0.2 miles up the Tremont Road. Turn into the Great Smoky Mountains Institute. Tour booklets are available in a box on the right. This two-way gravel road goes 3 miles to a turnaround as it parallels and crosses the Middle Prong of the Little River. Fishing, wading, and picnicking are fun on this auto trail that introduces the logging industry. The road can sometimes be closed in the winter.

In addition to the four guided auto tours, several roads are fun to truly see the Smokies. We suggest drives along the Little River Road between Gatlinburg and Townsend; Newfound Gap Road (US 441) between Cherokee and Gatlinburg; Clingmans Dome Road (off US 441 near Newfound Gap); Balsam Mountain Road off the Blue Ridge Parkway above Cherokee; the Foothills Parkway between US 321 at Walland and US 129 at Chilhowee Lake; the Foothills Parkway between US 321 in Wears Valley and US 321 at Walland; and the Foothills Parkway between US 321 near Cosby and I-40.

Two resources for driving through the Smoky Mountains are: *Smokies Road Guide: A Complete Guide to the Roads of Great Smoky Mountains National Park*, by Jerry DeLaughter, 1986.(Gatlinburg: Great Smoky Mountains Association, 1986), and Harry L. Moore, *A Roadside Guide to the Geology of the Great Smoky Mountains National Park*, by Harry L. Moore, 1988(Knoxville: University of Tennessee Press, 1988).

Both are available at the park visitor centers.

Waterfalls in the Smokies

Name	Roundtrip Distance	Area	Page in This Book
Roadside			
Laurel Creek Cascades		Cades Cove - Townsend	*
White Oak Flats		Cades Cove - Townsend	*
The Sinks		Elkmont - Metcalf Bottoms	*
Meigs Falls		Elkmont - Metcalf Bottoms	*
Mannis Branch Falls		Elkmont - Metcalf Bottoms	*
Place of a Thousand Drips		Gatlinburg - Mount LeConte	*
Noisy Creek Falls		Cosby	*
Flat Creek Falls		Cherokee	*
Hikes 0 to 2.5 Miles			
Crooked Arm Cascade	1.4 Miles	Cades Cove - Townsend	81
Spruce Flats Falls	1.9 Miles	Cades Cove - Townsend	73
Lynn Camp Prong Cascade	1.3 Miles	Cades Cove - Townsend	75
Laurel Falls	2.6 Miles	Elkmont - Metcalf Bottoms	50
Cataract Falls	0.7 Miles	Gatlinburg - Mt. LeConte	32
Mingo Falls	0.4 Miles	Cherokee - Deep Creek	99
Juney Whank Falls	0.6 Miles	Cherokee - Deep Creek	100
Toms Branch Falls	0.5 Miles	Cherokee - Deep Creek	100
Indian Creek Falls	1.6 Miles	Cherokee - Deep Creek	100
Twentymile Creek Cascade	1.25 Miles	Fontana	105
Hikes 2.6 to 5 Miles			
Abrams Falls	5 Miles	Cades Cove - Townsend	84
Upper Meigs Falls	3.6 Miles	Elkmont - Metcalf Bottoms	59
Jakes Creek Falls	3.2 Miles	Elkmont - Metcalf Bottoms	52

Name	Roundtrip Distance	Area	Page in This Book
Hikes 2.6 to 5 Miles (cont.)			
Huskey Branch Falls	4.3 Miles	Elkmont - Metcalf Bottoms	54
Grotto Falls	2.6 Miles	Gatlinburg - Mt. LeConte	35
Road Prong Falls & Cascades	2.6 & 3.3 Miles	Gatlinburg - Mt. LeConte	*
Baskins Creek Falls	3.2 Miles	Gatlinburg - Mt. LeConte	37
Fern Branch Falls	3.6 Miles	Gatlinburg - Mt. LeConte	27
Hen Wallow Falls	4.3 Miles	Cosby	17
Midnight Hole	2.8 Miles	Big Creek - Cataloochee	3
Mouse Creek Falls	4 Miles	Big Creek - Cataloochee	3
Chasteen Creek Falls	4 Miles	Cherokee - Deep Creek	*
Hikes 5.1 to 8 Miles			
Ramsey Cascades	8 Miles	Gatlinburg - Mt. LeConte	26
Rainbow Falls	5.5 Miles	Gatlinburg - Mt. LeConte	34
Indian Flats Falls	7.5 Miles	Cades Cove - Townsend	*
Sweat Heifer Cascades	7.3 or 7.6 Miles	Newfound Gap - Clingmans Dome or Cherokee - Deep Creek	*
Forney Creek Cascades	6 Miles	Newfound Gap - Clingmans Dome	*

* - Indicates Not In This Book

APPENDIX 4

Picnicking in the Smokies

Picnicking in the Smokies is a great experience. Many drive into the mountains to share a meal beside a stream or at a mountain vista. The national park maintains numerous picnic areas that have picnic tables, fire grates, and restrooms. Each has its own unique features that enhance a family picnic.

Cataloochee—Although Cataloochee can seem a bit out of the way, it is a wonderful spot for a picnic. Drive around to see the elk. Walk to some of the old buildings. Take a hike to the Woody House or on the Boogerman Trail. Or simply go to enjoy the day. No matter whether you come from Big Creek through the mountains or over Cataloochee Divide from Exit 20 on I-40, it's a pleasant experience.

Big Creek—A small picnic area near the Big Creek Campground is a favorite of fishermen and horseback riders. It is the perfect spot to stop on a trip through the mountains on I-40, or for a walk to Midnight Hole and Mouse Creek Falls. This is the picnic area that is closest to the interstate.

Welcome Centers on I-40—The Tennessee and North Carolina Welcome Centers, which are located on I-40 in the midst of the mountains, are good places for a picnic, to get information, and to use the restrooms. The North Carolina Welcome Center has a good view of the Pigeon River as it winds through the mountains.

Cosby—The picnic area is on the left before the campground. Cosby Creek can be heard in the woods below. This spot is rarely crowded. Walk on a guided nature trail or up to historic Mt. Cammerer. The trail to Albright Grove is not too far away.

Greenbrier—The Greenbrier section of the park is off US 321, 6 miles east of Gatlinburg. Picnic tables and a picnic shelter are located near the Middle Prong of the Little Pigeon River. Walk to Ramsey Cascades or simply get away from the crowds to this secluded valley. The road to Greenbrier can be closed in the winter.

Mynatt Park—This small Gatlinburg city park is on Airport Road a few blocks from downtown Gatlinburg. It is the site of a former Methodist church camp. Now picnickers can enjoy a moment beside the waters of LeConte Creek before going up to Cherokee Orchard and its many hikes.

Chimneys—This popular spot is on the Newfound Gap Road 5 miles beyond the Sugarlands Visitor Center. Tables are near the rushing Little Pigeon River, below the famed Chimney Tops. The Cove Hardwood Nature Trail originates at the picnic area. This is a good resting spot on a trip "over the top" or as a destination itself. The trailhead to Chimney Tops is 2.5 miles along the Newfound Gap Road.

Elkmont—This picnic area on the Little River, opposite the road, is paired with a popular year-round campground. The Elkmont area was once heavily logged and the site of a colony of vacation cabins and the Wonderland Hotel. The Elkmont Nature Trail and Huskey Branch Falls are nearby.

Metcalf Bottoms—Ten miles from Gatlinburg on the Little River Road, Metcalf Bottoms is located on the banks of the Little River. It is named for the Metcalf family who once lived in this area. Walk up to Little Greenbrier Schoolhouse and the Walker Sister's House or eat at the picnic area on your way between Gatlinburg and Townsend. This is very popular and can be crowded.

Cades Cove—This popular and often crowded picnic area is on the left as you enter Cades Cove. Arrive early to choose your table at the headwaters of Abrams Creek, which flows through Cades Cove. This is a good place for breakfast before you start the loop road or hike to Abrams Falls or Gregory Bald.

Tables on US 129 and NC 28—Picnic tables are located by the sides of US 129 and NC 28. These are excellent spots to rest from the twisting journey between Fontana and Maryville. Some have nice views of the Little Tennessee River or sit in pine forests. You may want to take advantage of these on the way to Twentymile Creek or to Fontana.

Look Rock—The campground and picnic area are on Chilhowee Mountain, 9.5 miles on the Foothills Parkway from US 321 at Walland, or 7 miles from US 129. This cooler spot is rarely crowded and is a nice place to rest before walking to the magnificent views from Look Rock Tower.

Fontana Dam—This picnic area is above Fontana Dam, which is the tallest dam in the Tennessee Valley Authority system. Picnic here and walk to Shuckstack Fire Tower, to Hazel Creek, or to the visitor center at the dam.

Collins Creek—Off the Newfound Gap Road, 6 miles north of Cherokee, this picnic area is filled with the sounds of Collins Creek as it tumbles past on its way to the Oconaluftee River. Named after Robert Collins, who guided Arnold Guyot into the mountains in the 1850s on surveying trips, it is near where Collins' home once stood. Collins was also gatekeeper and toll collector for the Oconaluftee Turnpike over the mountains. This picnic area is well located for a meal while visiting Cherokee, Oconaluftee Visitor Center, or Mingus Mill, or when hiking the Kephart Prong Trail.

Heintooga Overlook—This picnic area is located at the end of the Balsam Mountain Road, a spur off the Blue Ridge Parkway above Cherokee. You will eat at 5,535 feet above sea level. Walk to the overlook for views of the Oconaluftee Valley and the high Smokies. Combine this with a walk to Flat Creek or on the Balsam Mountain Nature Trail.

Deep Creek—This picnic area is paired with a nice campground above Bryson City on the banks of Deep Creek. Many go tubing on Deep Creek in the hot summer months. Walk to Juney Whank, Indian Creek, and Toms Branch Falls while you're in this scenic place.

Remember that picnics are for humans—not the wildlife. *Do not feed the wildlife!* It endangers their lives as well as your safety. Also, leave the picnic area clean, with all your trash properly disposed. These picnic spots are some of our favorites. Many other places lend themselves to a nice meal in the mountains.

Backpacking with Children

Over the years, we have enjoyed many outings with our children on both day and overnight trips. A lot of enjoyment can come from such trips, but a lot of disappointment is possible as well, especially on overnight trips. We would like to share a few tips that should help plan overnight trips and keep disappointments to a minimum. Keep in mind that every trip, like every family, is unique, so our tips are only suggestions—with the exception of safety precautions.

HELPFUL HINTS

- Never make an overnight trip your first experience with your child in the Smokies. It is a good idea to have several day hikes together before planning an overnight trip. This allows for experience, exposure to the outdoors, and evaluation of ability and enthusiasm.

- Pick a time when the weather is mild. Doing so will reduce the amount of clothing and types of equipment that you will need.

- Do not invest a lot in equipment until you "give it a try." It may be possible to borrow the needed gear.

- Choose a backcountry site that is easy to get to. There are several that are only 2 or 3 miles from the parking area.

- An overnight trip to a "front country" campground can be a valuable experience for both you and your children. Your children get the feel of sleeping outside in a tent, cooking outside, and the mountains at night, with the convenience of your car at hand.

- Plan ahead for things to keep your child interested. Knowledge of the area you are going to—points of interest, history, plants, and animals—is very helpful.

- Keep your menu simple, take food that is easy to prepare and that your child likes.

- Have a "Plan B," just in case the situation or the weather is not as you expected.

- Always expect rain in the Smokies.

THINGS TO DO FOR OVERNIGHT TRIPS

Always check with the National Park Service, either at a visitor center or the Backcountry Information Office. They have great advice and can make reservations and instruct you on regulations. Always obtain your permit before heading into the backcountry.

- Always tell someone where you are going, when you are leaving, and when to expect you back.

- Obtain a copy of backcountry regulations and follow them, especially for proper food storage.

- Always hang your pack and food on the cable system provided at backcountry sites.

- Always treat the water.

- If you pack it in, pack it out. Leave no trace!

Resources

RESOURCES BY THE AUTHORS

Going Along to Great Smoky Mountains National Park, by Charles W. Maynard, 2008. A colorful introduction to the park with illustrations, pictures, charts, stories, and many fun facts.

Waterfalls of the Smokies, by Hal Hubbs, Charles Maynard, and David Morris, 1992. A guide to over 40 waterfalls in Great Smoky Mountains National Park, fully illustrated with photographs.

Churches of the Smokies, by Charles W. Maynard. A booklet on the seven church buildings still in the park.

Hiking Trails of the Smokies, by Multiple Authors including David Morris and Charles Maynard. This is a comprehensive guide to all the maintained trails in Great Smoky Mountain National Park.

NONFICTION

Most of the following resources are available at the visitor centers in the Great Smoky Mountains National Park or online at https://www.smokies information.org/store.

The Cades Cove Story, by A. Randolph Shields, 1977. A short history of the settlement of Cades Cove.

Cades Cove: The Life and Death of a Southern Appalachian Community, by Durwood Dunn, 1988. An extensive study of the Cades Cove Community.

Cataloochee Valley-Vanished Settlement of the Great Smoky Mountains, by Hattie Caldwell Davis. A historical look at Cataloochee by one who was born there.

The Cherokees, by Grace Steele Woodward, 1963. A good history of the Cherokee.

Exploring the Smokies, by Rose Houk, 1989. A beautiful book offering many suggestions on how best to enjoy the Great Smoky Mountains National Park.

The French Broad, by Wilma Dykeman, 1992. An excellent and readable history of the region around the French Broad River.

Great Smoky Mountains Association Booklets on the Churches of the Smokies, the Civilian Conservation Corps, Walker Valley, the Walker Sisters, Grist Mills, and Log Cabins.

Great Smoky Mountains Association Guidebooks on Trees, Reptiles and Amphibians, Ferns, Wildflowers, Historic Buildings, Birds, Trails, Butterflies & Moths, and Waterfalls.

National Park Service film at Sugarlands Visitor Center near Gatlinburg.

National Park Service literature and brochures (Most have a minimal cost.)

Our Southern Highlanders: A Narrative of Adventure in the Southern Appalachians and a Study of Life Among the Mountaineers, by Horace Kephart, Reprint, 1976. A classic, written in the early 1900s, by someone who worked to establish the park.

Scavenger Hike Adventures: Great Smoky Mountains National Park, by Kat and John LaFevre, 2007. A fun guide to the park, with many adventurous scavenger hunts.

Smokies Guide: The official newspaper of Great Smoky Mountains National Park, by Great Smoky Mountains Association.

Smokies Life Magazine. A wonderful magazine with great articles and photographs on all aspects of the Great Smoky Mountains history, natural history, and people. Numerous issues are available.

The Smokies Yukky Book, by Doris Gove, 2006. An illustrated guide for children on the "weird, creepy, and completely gross stuff that really, really happens" in the Smokies.

Strangers in High Places: The Story of the Great Smoky Mountains, Expanded Edition, by Michael Frome, 1994. A good history of the Great Smoky Mountains.

The Trail of Tears: The Rise and Fall of the Cherokee Nation, by John Ehle, 1988. A well-written account of the removal.

Trails Illustrated Maps, by National Geographic Maps. The most up-to-date maps, with notes on the trails and the park.

The Troublesome Cub in the Great Smoky Mountains, by Lisa Horstman, 2001. The true story of a cub that ended up in the trash. A good message with great illustrations.

Venture to the Smokies: A Teddy Bear Explores Great Smoky Mountains National Park, by Sloan Heermance, 2007. A whimsical guide to the park as seen through the eyes of a teddy bear. Many activities are included.

Women of the Smokies: No Place for the Weary Kind, by Courtney Lix. A study of women of the Smokies who made significant contributions to the park and the surrounding area.

FICTION

Cataloochee: A Novel, by Wayne Caldwell, 2007. A novel of life in Cataloochee Valley from 1864 to 1928.

The Cherokee Crown of Tannassy, by William O. Steele, 1977. An early history of the Cherokee.

Cold Mountain: A Novel, by Charles Frazier, 1997. A novel about the Civil War in the mountains.

The Great Smoky Mountain Salamander Ball, by Lisa Horstman, 1997. A story in verse about the many salamanders of the park, with wonderful illustrations.

The Tall Woman, by Wilma Dykeman, 1962. A great story of post–Civil War mountain life by a well-known author of the region.

Thirteen Moons: A Novel, by Charles Frazier, 2006. A novel about Cherokee Removal in the mountains.

When I Was Young in the Mountains, by Cynthia Rylant, 1982. A beautifully illustrated book about life in the mountains years ago. A good book to read to young children.

Hike Index

Hike	Winter	Fall	Summer	Spring	Grassy Bald	Tower	Creeks	Historic Bldg/Sites	Old Growth Forest	Scenic Views	Waterfall	Teen	Elementary	Preschool	Hours	Miles
Big Creek – Cataloochee																
1. Midnight Hole & Mouse Creek Falls			*	*			*				*		*		4/5	4
2. Mount Sterling		*	*	*		*				*		*	*		5/6	5.4
3. Little Cataloochee	*	*	*	*			*	*				*	*		4	5.4
4. Boogerman Loop			*	*			*	*	*			*			5/7	7.7/9.8
5. Woody House			*	*			*	*					*		1.5/2	2
6. Cataloochee Valley Walk	*	*	*	*			*	*		*		*	*	*	4/5	8.4 or Less
Cosby																
7. Hen Wallow Falls		*	*				*				*		*		2/3	4.3
8. Mount Cammerer		*		*		*		*		*		*			6/7	11
9. Albright Grove		*		*					*				*		4/5	6.8
Gatlinburg – Mount LeConte																
10. Ramsey Cascades	*	*	*	*			*		*	*	*	*	*		5.5/7	8
11. Porters Creek Trail & Fern Branch Falls			*	*			*	*			*		*		2/3	2 & 3.6

Hike	Miles	Hours	Preschool	Elementary	Teen	Waterfall	Scenic Views	Old Growth Forest	Historic Bldg/Sites	Creeks	Tower	Grassy Bald	Spring	Summer	Fall	Winter
12. Gatlinburg Trail	4	2	*	*					*	*			*	*	*	*
13. Sugarlands Valley	0.5	30/45 min	*						*	*			*	*	*	*
14. Old Sugarlands	3-4	3		*	*				*	*			*	*	*	*
15. Cataract Falls	1	1	*			*							*	*		*
16. Twin Creeks	4.4	2/3		*					*	*			*	*	*	*
17. Rainbow Falls	5.5	3/4		*	*	*			*					*		*
18. Grotto Falls & Brushy Mountain	2.6 & 6.8	3 & 6	*	*		*	*			*			*		*	Cl.
19. Baskins Creek Falls	3 & 3.4	4		*	*	*			*				*			
20. Chimney Tops	3.5	4/5		*			*			*			*	*		
21. Alum Cave and Arch Rock to Mount LeConte	11	8/9	*	*	*		*			*			*	*		
Elkmont – Metcalf Bottoms																
22. Laurel Falls – Cove Mountain Fire Tower	2.6 & 8	2 & 5	*	*	*	*	*	*		*	*		*		*	
23. Jakes Creek Falls	3.2	3		*		*			*	*			*	*		

Hike	Miles	Hours
24. Little River and Cucumber Gap	6	4/5
25. Huskey Branch Falls	4.3	2.5/3
26. Curry Mountain	7	4/5
27. Little Greenbrier School and Walker Sister's House	4	3/3.5
28. Upper Meigs Falls	3.6	2/3
Newfound Gap – Clingmans Dome		
29. Charlies Bunion and the Jumpoff	10	6/7
30. Clingmans Dome	1	45 min/1
31. Andrews Bald	4.2	3/4
Cades Cove–Townsend		
32. Chestnut Top	1	1.5/2
33. Spruce Flats Falls	2	1.5/2
34. Lynn Camp Prong	1.5	1.5/2
35. Schoolhouse Gap, Turkeypen Ridge, Finley Cane, and Bote Mountain Loop	8.8	5/6
36. John Oliver Place	0.5/3	1/3
37. Rich Mountain Loop	8.7	5/6
38. Spence Field	10.6	7/8

Hike	Miles	Hours	Preschool	Elementary	Teen	Waterfall	Scenic Views	Old Growth Forest	Historic Bldg/Sites	Creeks	Tower	Grassy Bald	Spring	Summer	Fall	Winter
39. Elijah Oliver Place	1	1/1.5		*					*	*			*	*	*	*
40. Abrams Falls	5	3		*		*				*				*		Cl.
41. Gregory Bald	11	6/8		*	*		*					*	*	*		Cl.
42. Look Rock Tower	1	30 min/1	*	*			*				*		*	*	*	
Cherokee–Deep Creek																
43. Kephart Prong	4	3.5/4	*	*			*		*	*			*	*		
44. Smokemont Loop	3.4 & 6	2 & 4	*	*						*			*	*	*	
45. Oconaluftee Cherokee (Bi-Lingual)	4	1.5/2	*	*					*				*	*		Cl.
46. Flat Creek	5.2	3	*	*		*				*			*	*		*
47. Mingo Falls	0.5	30/45 min	*	*		*				*			*	*	*	*
48. Juney Whank Falls	0.6	1	*	*		*				*			*	*		
49. Indian Creek Falls	2	2	*	*		*			*	*			*	*	*	
50. Goldmine Loop	3	1.5/2		*						*			*	*		
Fontana																
51. Twentymile Creek Cascade	1.25	1/1.5	*	*		*				*			*	*		*
52. Shuckstack Fire Tower	7	6			*		*				*		*	*	*	

Mileage Chart

Gatlinburg							
34	Cherokee						
22	54	Townsend					
20	54	42	Cosby				
41	74	20	60	Maryville			
25	56	9	45	29	Cades Cove		
64	44	42	84	64	51	Fontana	
8	42	15	28	35	24	57	Pigeon Forge